Keep the Change

Mark Wagner, *Comedy & Tragedy*, 2013

KEEP THE CHANGE

A COLLECTOR'S TALES

of

LUCKY PENNIES, *COUNTERFEIT* C-NOTES,

and other

CURIOUS CURRENCY

Harley J. Spiller

PRINCETON ARCHITECTURAL PRESS · NEW YORK

Published by
Princeton Architectural Press
37 East Seventh Street
New York, New York 10003

Visit our website at www.papress.com

⟹⟸

Editor: Sara E. Stemen
Designer: Jan Haux

⟹⟸

Special thanks to: Meredith Baber, Sara Bader, Nicola Bednarek Brower,
Janet Behning, Erin Cain, Megan Carey, Carina Cha, Andrea Chlad, Tom Cho,
Barbara Darko, Russell Fernandez, Jan Cigliano Hartman, Diane Levinson,
Jennifer Lippert, Katharine Myers, Jaime Nelson, Rob Shaeffer, Marielle Suba,
Kaymar Thomas, Paul Wagner, Joseph Weston, and Janet Wong of
Princeton Architectural Press —Kevin C. Lippert, publisher

Library of Congress Cataloging-in-Publication Data
Spiller, Harley J.
Keep the change : a collector's tales of lucky pennies, counterfeit C-notes, and
other curious currency / Harley J. Spiller. — First edition.
pages   cm
Includes bibliographical references.
ISBN 978-1-61689-256-2 (paperback : alkaline paper)
1. Coins—Collectors and collecting—Anecdotes. 2. Bank notes—Collectors
and collecting—Anecdotes. 3. Spiller, Harley J.—Anecdotes. 4. Mutilated
coins—Anecdotes. 5. Counterfeits and counterfeiting—Anecdotes. 6. Numismatics—Anecdotes. 7. Curiosities and wonders—Anecdotes. I. Title.
CJ101.S65 2015
737—dc23
201402250

For people who pass along passion,
especially Dad and his Dad

Excerpt from the US Code of Federal Regulations,
concerning the reproduction of US currency

Notwithstanding any provision of chapter 25 of
Title 18 of the US Code, authority is hereby given for
the printing, publishing or importation, or the making
or importation of the necessary plates or items for
such printing or publishing, of color illustrations
of US currency provided that:

(1) The illustration be of a size less than three-
fourths or more than one and one-half, in linear
dimension, of each part of any matter so illustrated;

(2) The illustration be one-sided; and

(3) All negatives, plates, positives, digitized storage
medium, graphic files, magnetic medium, optical storage
devices, and any other thing used in the making of
the illustration that contain an image of the
illustration or any part thereof shall be destroyed
and/or deleted or erased after their final use in
accordance with this section.

31 C.F.R. §411 (2011)

CABINET OF CONTENTS

Introduction · 11

1

Up Like a Bad Penny

The Irresistible Force of Copper · 20

2

In Sam I Trust

US Federal Banknote Errors · 26

3

Sneak Thieves

A Bit about Clipping · 34

4

Fine Line

The Art of Money · 38

5

Case No. 6-02848

The Law · 50

6

A Hole in Your Pocket

Intentionally Burned Money · 58

7

Honest Wear

The Discovery of an Anticounterfeiting Secret · 64

8

Hamilton, Franklin, Biv, Juror, and Golden

Colorful Men of Money · 72

9

Frogskins and Cartwheels

Nicknames for Money · 82

10

Illustrated Taxonomy

and Glossary of Mutilated Money · 86

Notes · 103 / Further Reading · 108 /
Credits · 110 / Acknowledgments · 111 /
About the Author · 112

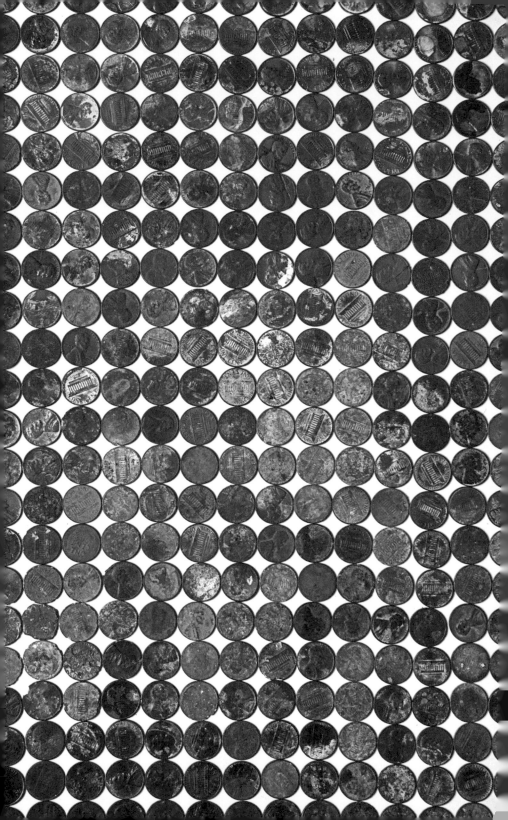

*"I must lie down where all the ladders start
In the foul rag and bone shop of the heart."*
—W. B. Yeats, "The Circus Animals' Desertion," 1939

WHAT a strange thing we humans have invented: money. Before that, we exchanged assets. Now we barter with currency, the icons of social covenants and governing authorities. Our largest denominations are mass-produced slips of cloth. Coins made of precious metal are no longer in general circulation. Our money is ephemeral by nature, subject to erosion, and fundamentally worthless, but oh, what we do to get it! And oh, what we do to it! {**Fig. 1**}

Most coin collectors abhor damage, frown on cleaning and artificial retoning, and prefer brilliant, imperfection-free coins straight from the mint. Patina, the surface appearance of things grown beautiful with age or use, is prized, and discoloration or staining is frowned upon, but to me, the two are the same. I admire collectors who ignore defects when face-to-face with rarities. I have nothing against new money—I'm just more enamored of the bottom of the grading categories used by serious collectors, the heavily worn and pitted, the blobs and discolored specimens. I love lumps of metal that can barely be identified (known to collectors by the grade "basal state") and collect singular mangled coins and bills that "create tension because they demand a creative response."[1]

Fig. 1

Found mangled quarter

WHO but the least imaginative, when examining a prized artifact, has not experienced flights of fancy like the following, which appeared in the *American Journal of Numismatics* in 1867:

> Every coin or medal of historic interest is a potent talisman:—to evoke the past and people it with resuscitated life, to secure the present against oblivion, and give earthly immortality to its heroes. The owner of a numismatic cabinet is a necromancer and a ruler of the spirits, and can fill, at pleasure, his lonely chamber with shapes of the departed, and majestic phantasms.[2]

That's high-flown prose, but it's also an incisive anticipation of the field that most informs this book: material culture studies, the examination through artifacts of societal beliefs, of values, ideas, attitudes, and assumptions.[3]

Numismatists are material culturists who ask, "What's in your cabinet?" and gauge each other by the replies. I didn't know that secret handshake in 1965, when I started collecting pennies, and still didn't know it in 1981, when I began my career in museums and spotted something out of place in the subbasement of the well-known institution where I worked: a broken-legged chest with greasy screws and bolts lying haphazardly in its velvet-lined drawers. The museum had just reinstalled its coins in custom Formica and Plexiglas cases, rendering obsolete the original wood, gilt, and glass exhibition furniture. I reported the situation to the administrator, who said, "You want it? Just get it out of here." I did as I was told, and am now the keeper of a restored nineteenth-century French numismatic cabinet. { **Fig. 2** }

Fig. 2

Mahogany is the timber of choice for long-term storage
and display of coins because of all woods it contains
the least amount of coin-damaging oils and resins.
This mahogany numismatic cabinet is of bombé form,
bearing gilt bronze decorative mounts with acanthus and
ribbon ornamentation. It is fitted with twelve dark-
green, velvet-lined trays, and a hinged serpentine top
with sliding beveled-glass vitrine, all raised on
cabriole legs ending in scrolled feet.

Generations of my family have worked such cast-offs for all their worth. After a day's labor and a hearty supper, my grandfather would often drive his horse and buggy around town, scavenging discarded couches and chairs. Neighbors assumed the Spillers were a dirty lot, but my family wasn't sitting on the foul furniture. They were burning its wood in the stove, salvaging the upholstery for rags, and digging into its crannies for lost valuables such as scissors, eyeglasses, and coins.

I was thirteen when a younger cousin bet me ten dollars on who would be taller when he turned twenty-one. I won, but then he offered a new bet: fifty dollars on who would be taller when I turned fifty. Certain I'd be stooped over by then, I started saving mutilated money to needle him a little at payoff time. I ended up a fraction of an inch taller and doubly happy, for I've come to see the eleven-plus pounds of mutilated money I amassed as a thing of beauty. What started as a lark has become a treasure. (Cousin Kenny also experienced a change of heart over the long course of the two bets. After less than one year as an assistant district attorney, he left the law for the scrap metal business.)

WHERE can't I find money for my collection?[4] Mutilated money can be anywhere. I love the hunt, the wait for the next breaching, the harpooning of the oxymoronic "better mutilation." I thrill to the serendipitous discovery of mangled money, whether it is coaxed out of its camouflage within a muddy tree bed or dusty corner or found smack in the middle of a road, in the back of a cash register, or in a lumpy envelope with a lighthearted note mailed by a friend who can't get my collection out of his head. { **Fig. 3** } There are others interested in mutilated money, and I've come to realize my pursuits are less rarefied than I'd supposed, less odd than Odyssean.

Currency-collage artist and collector Mark Wagner agrees. As he wrote to me in August 2013, "My chief pleasure here is that it is a point where the whole point of money falls apart....Money is supposed to be a substance where only quantity matters. As a unit of exchange it is supposed to be completely fungible, with any specimen of money capable of replacing any other specimen of money. But for us it is not."[5]

WHY have I chosen to focus on the idiosyncrasies of mutilated money? Because compiling a set that can never be completed provides an endless source of new knowledge. Because it's a field largely unrestrained by financial considerations. Because I can set my own standards. Because mutilation, corrosion, and erosion can make new money seem as venerable as the most ancient. My collection also doubles as a self-enforced rainy-day reserve (if a bill or coin is beat up enough, I will keep it rather than spend it). Mangled money collecting is not about the control prized by most collectors—it is about the future, about the unanticipatable surprise of finding new and different types of alterations. I see my collection as a cache that cannot be counted in standard ways. It's not about money; it's about what can be learned from money.

WHEN does money fall apart? There are many answers, most labyrinthine. All humans, even brilliant financial experts, can become overwhelmed by money, more so by the lack of it. Money is always in flux, but it is here to stay. Knowledge is another type of currency, and educating ourselves about money is the best thing we can do. So, with the hope of enter-taining and enlightening, I present the true stories of filthy lucre that run in my bones.

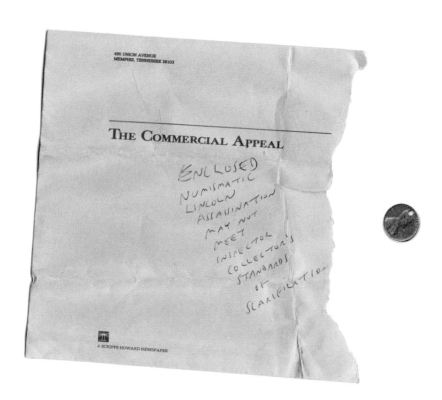

Fig. 3
Envelope and pierced cent mailed to me by a good
friend. (I present museum education programs under the
name Inspector Collector.)

Mr. Richard Buckley, the financial manager for my parents' company, was one of five brothers who all became accountants. He was also a serious numismatist who gave me wise collecting counsel and, once, a folder of Liberty nickels. These were, to an eight- or nine-year-old kid, ancient and rare. My eyes lit up, but Mr. Buckley assured me their fiscal value was low because of their poor condition. Still, this gift of disfigured coins from a traditional, waxed-shoelace kind of man has always captivated me. Each of the sixteen coins is more than a century old; all are worn smooth. The 1906 five-cent piece has black, brown, red, rust, and celadon-colored corrosion. The 1909 example is blackened and scuffed in a unique manner. I imagine it caught under a buggy wheel, careening around cobblestones.

UP LIKE A BAD PENNY

The Irresistible Force of Copper

The pale sea curdled on the shingle and the
green tower of the Metropole looked like a dug-up
coin verdigrised with age-old mould.
—Graham Greene, *Brighton Rock*, 1938

COPPER, THE ORIGINAL PENNY METAL, is found in the earth and in human bones, muscle, and liver. It is conductive of heat and electricity and has a legendarily warm reddish-orange color. {**Fig. 4**} Copper was considered sacred by the Mississippians, who lived from 800 to 1600 CE in central North America. They bartered for the malleable tawny ore and used it to create expressive repoussé (designs made by hammering on the reverse side of metal) plates and elite body ornamentation. Their most enduring legacy is the gigantic mounds in which they buried their dead with ritual copper plaques. Maybe they put copper back in the earth where it came from because that's where it's most powerful.

Fig. 4
This is my favorite verdigrised cent.

The prevailing culture was vastly different by 1787, when a private mint repurposed copper for currency and stamped the first cents in the United States. Those 100 percent copper pennies were sixty-three times heavier than today's cents, which are mainly zinc, clad with only one two-thousandths of an inch of copper.[1]

The US Mint opened in 1792 and soon produced its first coins: 11,178 copper cents so inelegant they were nicknamed "Liberty in Fright." It was not until 1862 that Congress declared copper to be legal tender, so these early cents couldn't be deposited with banks. They were used for small purchases and frequently tossed by merchants into barrels and sold in bulk to smelters, for repurposing; carpenters, to use as anchors for screws and nails; hoteliers, to smooth, pierce, number, and use as key tags; hunters, to notch for rifle sights; cooks, for fixing the color of pickles (people died: copper plus vinegar is deadly); and undertakers, for use in sealing the eyes of the dead.

Pennies were also drilled, strung, and carried to Africa to trade for slaves. Later, pennies were notched in precise locations and used by escaping slaves as bona fides on the Underground Railroad. Mourners of Abraham Lincoln turned pennies into souvenirs by placing them on railroad tracks to be flattened by his Springfield-bound funeral train.[2] Forty-four years later, on the centennial of his birth, Lincoln's profile replaced an allegorical feather-bonneted Indian, and Honest Abe became the first real person depicted on a US coin. Freighted with emancipatory significance, the Lincoln cent was an immediate and sustained national sensation.[3] By the end of 2012, 470,952,310,918 Lincoln cents had been minted.

One day in 1964 I was home sick from school, and my father sired a new pastime by tossing me a sack of pennies and a blue Whitman coin folder. I've enjoyed the hobby ever since, especially the search for uncommon coins. I knew I had proven my collecting mettle when, a few years later, Dad ceremoniously handed over a dented coffee can full of coins his father had gathered over a lifetime in Volochisk, Russia, his birthplace, and in his adopted hometown, LeRoy, New York.[4] Dad and I spent time learning numismatics and how to have fun with next to no money. Most memorably, he glued a penny to a tile floor outside my sisters' rooms so we could make merry when unsuspecting guests tried to pick it up.

In 1967 I was standing in front of Bakert's candy shop in Eggertsville, New York, when I first heard the siren ring of coins on concrete. I stared in disbelief as real money was tossed to the winds by insouciant, snack-slurping teens. I could hardly wait until they left to snap it up. Now, after almost fifty years of picking up lucky pennies, I'm reluctant to stoop for run-of-the-mint cents, particularly the nearly copper-free post-1982 lightweights, which barely click when dropped.

The highlights of my hoard include a penny bent over double, likely by a snowplow; one with its core excised; and some so bitten and chewed they must have been doused with corrosive chemicals. { Fig. 5 } I have yet to successfully dig a tire-smoothed beauty out of crosswalk tar but will do just about anything short of defying oncoming traffic to collect a coin showing unexampled marks of wear and tear.

The largest subset of my mutilated-money collection consists of pennies in various states of oxidation. Their gradated celadon tones recall both the Statue of Liberty's elegant

Fig. 5
Five uniquely and severely damaged cents

patina and Mark Rothko's late paintings, and they inspired artist Norm Magnusson to create a method for speeding penny oxidation: a box made of woven copper bands splashed with copper sulfate. { **Fig. 6**} The artist's intention is for coins left inside to develop the variegated greenish-blue patina called verdigris, a word stemming from *vert de Grèce*, the Old French term for the metallic green pigment crucial to ancient Greeks. While numismatists prize the pristine nature of beautifully made pieces of money, they also place value on naturally variegated patina.

In his authoritative book on large cents, *Penny Whimsy*, the numismatist William H. Sheldon describes how relatively pure pre-1815 copper pennies come in "rich shades of green, red, brown, yellow, and even deep ebony; together with blendings of these not elsewhere matched in nature save perhaps in autumn leaves."[5] The murky-colored coins I favor are more like decaying foliage in spring snowmelt.

Corrosion and erosion are just two of the ways in which cents suffer indignities. Thrift is another. Governments save

Fig. 6

This copper sulfate–splashed copper box by artist
Norm Magnusson is very slowly developing patina, but
cents left inside are not yet showing verdigris.

money by eliminating money, and, in the ultimate abuse, the
nations of Australia, Brazil, Canada, and Sweden have elim-
inated pennies altogether.[6] Even the US Mint demeans pennies, describing them as "minor coins."[7]

Still, there are many present-day nonfiscal uses for pennies: people have figured out how to use them as batteries,
algae retardants, and tire-tread checkers.[8] It's easy to turn
pennies into tap-shoe taps and hem weights. Pennies buried
in the garden yield more fulsome hydrangeas by increasing
the pH of the soil. They repel slugs, which can experience
electric shocks when they come into contact with copper and
zinc. There is also, of course, the age-old practice of tossing
pennies into wishing wells, where copper, zinc, and water
react to create all kinds of gorgeously muculent spots, speck-
les, and scars. Whether you prefer shiny new coins or bur-
nished old chestnuts, most would agree that etched marks in
copper are irresistible wrinkles of history, lasting pocks doc-
umenting the exertions of life.

CHAPTER

IN SAM I TRUST

US Federal Banknote Errors

IN 1995 I TOOK A JOB with the Gallery at Takashimaya, part of the New York City flagship of an international Japanese retail corporation that enjoyed fifteen billion dollars in sales that year. Designed by Philip Johnson, Takashimaya's elegant Fifth Avenue shop featured gold-leaf ceilings in an East-meets-West atmosphere. Unfortunately, unlike the Japanese, Westerners aren't accustomed to buying art in department stores, and the gallery foundered.

When I announced my resignation, a friend from accounting stopped by to wish me well. "I've got a present for you," he said, and I thought, "How nice," until he added, "Gimme fifty bucks."

My sudden joy evaporated. "C'mon, Sam, I know I work in art and you're in finance, but anyone knows that's not a present."

"Trust me," he whispered.

Sam was six feet four, a steely-eyed Albanian émigré. He must have been hired, at least in part, for his imposing presence—his job involved carrying cash, lots of it. Takashimaya, like other Japanese stores, did its best to provide change in clean, new currency to suggest that it was well prepared and deserving of customer confidence. (Rare is the Tokyo shopkeeper who would press crumpled yen into the hand of a valued customer.) It was Sam's responsibility to claim standing orders for thousands of new US bills. He regularly carried large sums through the midtown streets to his desk, where he counted and placed stacks of crisp cash in Takashimaya's tills.

Stunned by Sam's brass, I stared at him and reflected on our time as colleagues. He had never exhibited any cause for distrust, but was clearly enjoying making me squirm. I checked my wallet and found sixty-seven dollars, enough to meet his demand and still buy something for lunch.

I stared up at him one more time and forked over the fifty. At the same time, Sam handed me a small stack of singles. Without counting the bills, I sensed I'd been had and balked.

"Look carefully, curator," he snarked, and that's when my eyes popped. {Fig. 7}

I shot out of my chair and shook Sam's big hand in thanks. He smiled broadly and explained how he'd discovered the twelve uncirculated, sequentially numbered bills after his weekly bank run, replaced them with his own money, and set the misprints aside.

Lunch hour came, and I headed out the door—not to eat but to visit Stack's, the vaunted numismatics firm in business since 1935. I met with a stony-eyed clerk, who said, "Let's see what we've got here," pulled on cotton gloves, arrayed the bills on a velvet pad, and examined them through a jeweler's loupe. My heart started to race. It wasn't long before I heard, "I can offer you five hundred dollars right now."

"No, thank you," I replied, with my best poker face. My Brooklyn-born mom had instilled in me a wariness of big-city wiles, and alarms sounded in my head when I was offered ten times what I'd paid.

The next time I visited my hometown of Buffalo, I brought the misprinted money to local coin dealer Harold B. Rice, who followed the same numismatic ritual: white gloves, black velvet, fancy magnifier.

Harold, whom I'd known and trusted since age five, said, "Hmm" and took quite a while before offering "I can give you nine hundred dollars, cash."

Fig. 7

Sequentially numbered, erroneously printed
and issued one-dollar notes

Fig. 8
"Star note." These official error replacement
bills attract detail-oriented collectors.

"Uh...thanks, but no thanks," I replied, too stunned to part with my burgeoning windfall. Harold sold me archival sleeves, and I loaded up the insufficiently inked bills and placed them where they remain to this day: in a vault.

So what are these twelve one-dollar bills really worth? If I bring them to a bank, I'll get twelve standard dollars in exchange, so why did Stack's offer me five hundred dollars and Rice nearly double that? Because there are many collectors who vie to add such government mistakes to their holdings. (Collectors engaged in this alternative market develop heightened senses. They must be able to identify all types of mistakes, because there are even forgers who specialize in faking error currency.)

Controls for ensuring the precision of US currency are world-class, and squadrons of determined inspectors operating high-tech machines safeguard the Bureau of Engraving and Printing's most important product. Each bill is supposed to weigh exactly one gram and measure 2.61 inches wide by 6.14 inches long by 0.0043 inches thick. Defective currency is destroyed, and substitute bills with the same serial numbers are issued. These replacements are known as "star notes" because of the unique asterisks they carry at the ends of their serial numbers. {Fig. 8}

Hundreds of steps are needed to create US bills. In 2012, for example, more than eight billion rectangles of the government's proprietary fabric soaked up close to three thousand tons of ink to create just under three hundred and fifty-nine billion dollars. Such large numbers mean that mistakes can and do slip into circulation.

Miscut one-dollar note

Officially, misprinted money is worth no
more or less than its face value, but
competitive collectors invariably pay
more for numismatic rarities, and there
is a lively trade in "error bills," i.e.,
paper currency that is:

* miscut {see opposite}
* misaligned
* inverted
* smeared
* double inked
* overinked
* insufficiently inked
* missing ink
* printed over folds
* double-denominated (when, for example,
  a one-hundred-dollar obverse is
  printed with a one-dollar reverse)

CHAPTER

SNEAK THIEVES

A Bit about Clipping

Isaac Newton, famous for his work with gravity, is less well known for his ferocious role at England's Royal Mint. Fiscal disarray was rampant when Newton became warden in 1696 and the purity and genuineness of coins varied wildly. Thieves of the time "clipped" coins (snipped or shaved off bits to sell); used punches to steal precious metals (often masking their crimes by filling the holes with cheaper material); and "abstracted a little bullion with acids."[1] Ordinary people knew how to bite coins to gauge their malleability and ascertain the type of metal, and some carried scales to weigh coins and files to notch their edges and determine if coins were pure or plated. {Fig. 9} Newton, who saw the big picture in small details, set feverishly to establishing public trust in England's money.

Stealing and selling bits of precious coin metal were fairly inconspicuous schemes, at least until Sir Isaac's exactitude and knowledge of metallurgy (and alchemy) began shoring up mint operations. He brought in new machinery, helped demand a recall and meltdown of *all* extant coins, and struck a completely new series of round coins with strict weight and purity regulations.[2] Newton completed the massive recoining in just three years and was rewarded with a promotion to master of the royal mint, where he continued to bring order to finance by personally raiding taverns, interrogating suspects, and searching for clues in London's Newgate Prison (where the pirate Captain William Kidd was held). Newton's efforts to stabilize British society included urging the enforcement of the death penalty for crimes against the Crown's currency, and he was proud of having had many clippers and "coyners" hanged.[3]

One of Newton's important anticlipping innovations was edge milling, a process by which tiny ridges, known as

Fig. 9

Except for the top coin, which is a penny cinched
in what appears to be a foil cap from a liquor
bottle, I do not know how or why the edges of these
contemporary coins were altered.

reeds, are added to the rim of a coin. It wasn't until early in the twenty-first century that an improvement was made to Newton's reeds and the US Mint introduced coin edges inscribed in specific and consistent locations. Newton's technique is still in widespread use, and the edges of today's US dimes, quarters, halves, and dollars feature precise numbers of reeds: according to the US Mint, dimes have exactly 118; quarters, 119; half dollars, 150; and dollars, 189. (The reeds are too tiny for me to tally, so I'm forced to trust the mint's count.)

In the eighteenth and nineteenth centuries, it was customary to make change by cutting eight-*reales* coins into the fractional wedges of metal known as "pieces of eight." Though such practices were illegal, prosecution was rare. Altered coins wreaked havoc in the marketplace and led to bitter altercations, but at the time the public considered capital punishment too draconian a measure for tinkering with metal.

Ordinary people were not the only debasers of currency, though; nations also engaged in the practice. There has never been a government that could resist the temptation to bail itself out by making coins smaller and/or switching to less valuable metals. My favorite such brazen governmental act involved the silver eight *reales* coins minted for the Spanish Crown in colonial Guadalajara, Mexico. Soon after these coins were first released in 1821, Mexico declared its independence from Spain, and political instability shook the region. Eventually the fledgling government of Costa Rica nationalized all foreign coins, including the *reales*, by extracting precious metal from them and counterstamping them with its own coat of arms. It was thus that large, ragged holes were officially plugged out of one nation's coins to turn them into another nation's official currency.[4]

CHAPTER

FINE LINE

The Art of Money

SOME OF THE FINEST LINES in the art world today are those on US dollar bills. The US Department of the Treasury combines old-world engraving skills with modern machinery to create incredibly detailed notes that inspire confidence and deter illicit reproduction. The image below is an enlargement of five-eighths of one square inch of a dollar bill. {Fig. 10} Just the idea of reproducing all those curvy, tapering lines is daunting; still, the urge is irresistible to many.

"Shoving the queer" (nineteenth-century slang for passing counterfeit money) is the work of criminals. Artists have higher motivations for their imitations of money, aesthetics and social commentary chief among them. The first true-to-life re-creation of US money made for artistic (as opposed to deceitful) purposes was William Michael Harnett's 1877

Fig. 10
The engraving on US currency is fabulously complex.

painting of a tattered, ragged-edged five-dollar bill. Harnett chose banknotes for a subject because their flatness suited his passion for trompe l'oeil (French for "fools the eye") painting. He preferred depicting well-worn bills because of their intrinsic history; when he submitted *A Bad Counterfeit* to the National Academy of Design for review, the expert judges were so sure Harnett had pasted a real bill on a panel, they removed the glass frame to prove their contention.[1] They were wrong. Harnett was that good.

Hundreds of artists have followed Harnett's lead in the replication of money, many with more provocative intentions, including his friend John Haberle, who, like Harnett, was investigated by the Secret Service.[2] Another contemporary, Victor Dubreuil, had a painting of barrels full of cash confiscated and held behind bars at the Treasury until, under 1909 law, it was destroyed.[3] Dubreuil's paintings were not as realistic as Harnett's or Haberle's, but law enforcement was apparently very concerned about populists with precise rendering skills.

A fine line separates mutilation from art. A dollar covered in graffiti, for example, can be seen as good for nothing or, alternatively, as an artifact of stimulating complexity. By the time the nineteenth- and early twentieth-century passion for realistic paintings of cash died down, twentieth-century artists, including Marisol, Robert Rauschenberg, and Andy Warhol, were creating their own cheekily subverted dollars. The tradition continues with twenty-first-century artists such as Mark Wagner (see frontispiece), who desecrates dollars only to reinvest them with new value, symbolism, and wit. Wagner spends about one thousand dollars a year on his main art supply, one-dollar bills. He slices them into thin ribbons, sorts the bits by color (or the absence thereof), and creates often monumental collages. As Wagner writes, "Anarchists are certain I'm an anarchist because I cut up a favorite tool of the oppressor. Capitalists think I'm a capitalist because I revel in it."[4]

Back when dollars came more dearly to him, Wagner and a studio mate were discussing where to go for "linner," their only meal of the day. Wagner realized his billfold was empty and, famished and annoyed, began to grouse. Then Wagner's friend pointed out that there were spendable dollar bills on the worktable right in front of him, waiting to be used in his artwork. In Wagner's mind, the crisp, new bills had transformed from money to nonmoney and back again.[5]

Wagner's blinding focus is typical of altered-currency aficionados. As artist and collector of rubber- stamped bills Adamandia Kapsalis posted on Facebook: "I don't want the money, just the photos of stamps on the money. Hmm... did I just say I don't want money?"[6]

Today's most venerated money artist is J. S. G. Boggs. He doesn't mutilate currency; he makes incredibly detailed freehand illustrations of money, always adding or subtracting features so anyone giving more than a cursory glance will know they are fake. Boggs' deft acts of civil disobedience deconstruct the function and symbolism of money: he exchanges his drawings of banknotes for food and other necessities, and frames and exhibits the real money he insists on receiving in change. The Secret Service has several times confiscated Boggs's work and personal effects, but has never successfully prosecuted him for counterfeiting. Meanwhile, two and a half miles south of Secret Service headquarters, Boggs's art sits proudly in the national collection at the Smithsonian American Art Museum.

Back when Boggs was listed in the telephone book, I called and asked if he would be a guest teacher in my after-school museum-studies program. We struck a deal that he would be paid seventeen bucks: one hand-drawn bill per grade-schooler. Boggs came to New York and started his lesson by drawing a picture on the chalkboard and asking the students, "What is it?"

"A dog?"

"No."

"A dog sitting down?"

"No."

"A beagle?"

"No."

"A bear?"

"No."

This went on for fifteen minutes, until Boggs elicited the answer he sought:

"A picture of a dog."

Then he asked, "What's a dollar worth?"

"Four quarters?"

"No."

"Ten dimes?"

"No."

Another fifteen minutes elapsed before a child said, "I'd shovel snow for an hour to get a dollar." Boggs's Socratic method made everyone in the room realize that money is only a symbol—that dollars are worth different things to each of us.

Boggs likes to make people think new thoughts. He places value where it hasn't existed and makes art that one doesn't have to be rich to collect, just fortuitous. He also

Fig. 11

Beriah Wall, *Piggy Bank*, 2013

Fig. 12

Nicolás Dumit Estévez, *Cash Tendered*, 2003

Fig. 13

David Greg Harth, *I Am America*, 2012

Fig. 14

Peggy Diggs, series of rubber-stamped
one-dollar bills, 2003

knows that anyone can, for free or low cost, build an archive of cartoon dollars or Monopoly money. I save such "flash" (play) money and showed some to the kids and Boggs, who asked if he could buy my collection. Was this another of Boggs's provocative tests? I might never know, because I declined without even asking what he was offering. I've lost contact with Boggs, but one thing is certain: his final question came an hour too late. Selling my collection would have flown in the face of the lesson he'd just imparted.

Sculptor Beriah Wall avoids breaking the law by making coins out of clay instead of metal.[7] By using text sparingly on his coins and placing them around town for people to find, he ensures his work is open to numerous interpretations. {Fig.11} Performance artist Nicolás Dumit Estévez demonetizes dollars by placing them in glassine envelopes, sealing and signing the flaps, and selling them with the caveat that bills removed from the envelopes will no longer "be recognized as art by the artist or any party involved in the sale."[8] According to Estévez, if you take the dollar out of the envelope it is no longer art but merely another dollar worth one hundred cents. I purchased my one-dollar bill, {Fig.12} part of an edition of ninety-nine, for ninety-nine cents. Art propagandist David Greg Harth achieves wide circulation by rubber-stamping bills with bold political squibs, {Fig.13} as does artist Peggy Diggs, who inks the cream margin along the edges of bills with essential questions such as "What do you think is gained in poverty and lost through wealth?" {Fig.14} Jim Costanzo, artist and founder of the Aaron Burr Society (which practices nonviolent resistance to authorities it believes has stolen money from the public), also creates socially pointed art, rubber-stamping and spending real

Fig. 15
Jim Costanzo, *Free Money*, April 1, 2009

bills with bold, red slogans such as "Free Money." {Fig. 15} Some of Costanzo's objectives mirror those of the Occupy Wall Street movement and might be accomplished by instead totally destroying money, but messages like his travel best when emblazoned on US cash.

Gülşen Çalık, a Turkish conceptual artist living in New York City, took another approach to the manipulation of the value of cash with *How to Make a Buck*, an artwork she spent ten years creating. During that time, Çalık removed one very narrow strip from each of more than one hundred twenty-dollar bills. She taped each bill back together, minus the strip, and returned it to circulation. Then she made a composite bill from the stolen strips, a "new" twenty-dollar bill. {Fig. 16}

Çalık's decade-long moneymaking process made her very nervous, so she calmed herself by logging receipts for each banknote she sent back into circulation. During the process she learned a lot about the composition of money, including the fact that, despite the Bureau of Engraving and

Fig. 16

Gülşen Çalık, *How to Make a Buck*, 1999–2009

Printing's best efforts, the size of the dollar's rectangle differs from bill to bill. About this literal margin of error, Çalık says, "I could have taken a ruler and a sharp knife and trimmed the edges to perfection, but that would have been unwise." Çalık believes "the 'beauty' of the work is also about its integrity as an honest metaphor for the labor and exchange of the bill; the exchange of work for a splice of currency." [9] Çalık found a new way to make money, but rather than spend it, she chooses to live with it; *How to Make a Buck* is not for sale.

Artists aren't the only people who mutilate currency. Bureaucrats, soldiers, spies, magicians, tinkerers, and citizens of every stripe engage in the seemingly irresistible compulsion. Why? To send the world messages about power and patriotism, terrorism and aesthetics, ethics, economics, greed, creed, science, politics, altruism, hatred, ego, and so on. Mutilating money is a thinking person's gambit; the act is driven by as many motivations as there are people who tread the enticing and shaky line between legality and illegality.

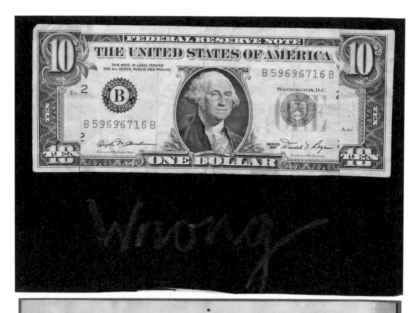

MY FIRST JOB IN NEW YORK WAS AS
A STREET VENDOR, SELLING ITALIAN
ICES. I DIDN'T NOTICE THIS UNUSUAL
TEN-DOLLAR BILL UNTIL I WAS COUNT-
ING UP THE DAY'S TAKE. SINCE MY
CUT WAS 25%, I LOOKED AT IT THIS
WAY: I HAD INVOLUNTARILY PAID
$2.50 FOR A PIECE OF SOMEONE'S
ART WORK.

A MONTH LATER A THIN MAN WITH HIS
JAW WIRED SHUT BOUGHT AN ITALIAN
ICE WITH A $20 BILL. BY THIS TIME,
I HAD LEARNED TO CHECK ALL 10'S
AND 20'S CLOSELY AND RECOGNIZED
THIS ARTIST'S PARTICULAR STYLE.
"NO, THANKS!" I SAID, THROWING HIS
20 AT HIM AND GRABBING MY ICE,
SIMULTANEOUSLY.

SOME PEOPLE QUESTION HOW ONE CAN
PROFIT BY MAKING SUCH BILLS. THE
ANSWER IS THAT A TEN-DOLLAR BILL
WITHOUT ONE END BUT WITH BOTH
SERIAL NUMBERS CAN BE EXCHANGED
AT THE BANK. THE 2 ENDS ARE NOT
FROM THE SAME BILL. IT MAY SEEM
LIKE A LOT OF BOTHER FOR $9 OR
$19, BUT I GEUSS IT'S HARD TO GO
ON JOB INTERVIEWS WITH YOUR JAW
WIRED SHUT.   -IRIS ROSE

Iris Rose, *Wrong*, 1983

You can learn a lot from fakes,
like the one used by artist Iris Rose
in Wrong, her 1983 piece about her
experiences with a counterfeiter.
We, the people, Rose intimates in this
piece of physical evidence/documentation
of her postmodern performative work,
are on the front lines of fiscal
malpractice. We must use our experience
and due diligence to protect ourselves.

CHAPTER

CASE NO. 6-02848

The Law

Non olet.

(Money does not smell.)[1]

MONEY CARRIES COMPLEX MEANINGS far and wide, and people everywhere circulate ideas by altering their cash. Federal laws prohibit marking banknotes, but if the authorities prosecuted every case, would Secretary of the Treasury John W. Snow have taken pen and ink and signed a bill above his engraved signature? {Fig. 17} Was Snow's act illegal, or was it OK because of his position of power? Is it illegal for ordinary people—a grandparent, say—to write "Happy Birthday" on a cash gift? A federal law makes mutilation of any "national bank obligation" a crime:

> Whoever mutilates, cuts, defaces, disfigures, or perforates, or unites or cements together, or does any other thing to any bank bill, draft, note, or other evidence of debt issued by any national banking association, or Federal Reserve bank, or the Federal Reserve System, with intent to render such bank bill, draft, note, or other evidence of debt unfit to be reissued, shall be fined under this title or imprisoned not more than six months, or both. 18 U.S.C. §333

If the authorities pursued every occurrence of monetary mutilation, your grandfather might be sharing a cell with the former secretary of the treasury. But enforcement and prosecution of the code hinge on one key word: *intent*. Happily, the spirit of the law sometimes triumphs over the letter. If

Fig. 17
One-dollar bill autographed by John W. Snow,
seventy-third US secretary of the treasury

your actions are *well intended*, a case brought against you will likely be quashed.

When was the last time a teacher believed a student who claimed "The dog ate my homework"? If, however, Fido mauls your money, not all is lost. There exists within the *matryoshka* doll–like Department of the Treasury a Bureau of Engraving and Printing with an Office of Currency Standards, wherein nests a Mutilated Currency Division, which inspects and provides reimbursement for damaged US currency. The division handles some thirty thousand claims per year, mostly bills compromised by flood or fire. The BEP also has an Office of External Relations with public affairs specialists, one of whom informed me in 2013 that "the redemption program has been inundated with claims from recent global disasters."[2] US currency has never been demonetized (deprived of its fiscal value). No matter where on earth you find yourself and your money, no matter how high the water or how deep the hole, your greenbacks are guaranteed.

In 2009 the *Washington Post* reported a stunning story of redemption. A Texas customs broker and two associates surfaced with $6.4 million in bills so water-damaged they were fused into bricks.[3] Federal investigators called their stories "conflicting and cockamamy" and suspected they were after the gold standard of money laundering: a government reimbursement check. Wrongdoing couldn't be proven, though, and an out-of-court monetary settlement was eventually reached.

Something similar happened to me. Well, more along the lines of Beethoven's merry rondo "Rage Over a Lost Penny, Vented in a Caprice."[4] In the autumn of 1995 I spied some partially concealed treasure: a pair of engravings of Andrew Jackson stuck in the metal saddle of a taxi door. "Whoopee," I thought, "forty scoots," until I snatched them up and realized that the beguiling portraits of President Jackson were all that was left of the two twenties. Conflicted between keeping the fragments and exploring how the reimbursement process works, I saved one snippet and submitted the other.

A few months later I received a reply from the manager of yet another Treasury office, the Claims Processing Division, indicating my request had been assigned Case No. 6-02848. I was politely instructed that "the portion of the note submitted must measure clearly more than one-half of the original whole note, in order to receive payment."[5] (Otherwise crooks would rip bills in half, turn them in separately, and the Feds would end up paying out double.)[6] My portion measured well under one-half, and therefore it could not be exchanged. (There was no mention of what was done with the scrap I submitted—it was probably shredded.) The letter, typed on elegant cream Crane & Co. stationery with watermarked eagles and stars, was signed in ink by Queen McBride, who concluded, on a reassuring note, "Our office stands ready to be of assistance to you on another occasion."[7]

A few years later I took Ms. McBride up on her kind offer when I got a one-dollar bill missing an inch or two from its right-hand side. Six months or so later, long after I'd forgotten about the partial dollar, I came home to a letter from the US Department of the Treasury's Financial Management Service's Regional Financial Center in Philadelphia. Through the envelope's clear plastic window I saw my name and address on an IRS-esque notice. "Oh no," I flinched, "another audit." Fortunately it was only the reimbursement for the torn bill I'd submitted, in the form of a check from the Treasury's Kansas City, Missouri, office. The memo section of the check included the code "N/A," an internal Treasury notation "meaning there were no discrepancies or shortages in the amount redeemed versus the amount claimed."[8]

The United States keeps a fastidious eye on its money. The system works, and our money really *is* guaranteed. But at what cost? My request to replace a measly buck had gone from New York City through Washington, DC, to Kansas City to Philadelphia and back to New York. How many federal workers, besides the regional disbursal officer whose printed signature appears on the check, does it take to process such returns? How much does it cost to design, produce, prepare, and mail the multicolored Treasury check with its anti-counterfeiting Quick Response code and hidden fluorescent fibers? How much more will it cost because of my decision to keep the check rather than cash it, forcing a federal book-keeper to eventually cancel the reimbursement and reconcile the books?

These painstaking efforts to honor the dollar's guarantee give the public faith and uphold the value of US currency the world over. No matter what harm befalls a greenback, it can be submitted to the US Department of the Treasury and will, whenever appropriate, be replaced. (If only similar recompense could be made to the student whose homework really does get eaten by a dog.)

* * *

The US Mint, yet another division of the Treasury, promotes similar confidence in its money by redeeming "bent, broken, corroded, not whole, melted together, and not machine count-able" coins. Such mutilated coins are no longer accepted at face value, though—their redemption is based on the weights of their various metals. Coins that have suffered lesser degrees of damage are categorized as "uncurrent." Such read-ily identifiable and machine-countable coins are redeemed by consumer banks.

Once I sent a mangled penny back to the mint. I never got a response, so I checked the regulations carefully and learned there are substantial minimum weights for mutilated-coin redemption. My penny was infinitesimal compared to the truckloads of coin-redemption shipments that started coming from China in 2008 to a private reimbursement con-tractor in Cedar Rapids, Iowa. Surprisingly, a vast majority of the coins were undamaged. The Treasury's Office of the Inspector General questioned the shippers but was unable to elicit any plausible or verifiable explanation. *Coin World* magazine submitted a Freedom of Information Act request and discovered that the shippers were probably conducting these international operations to avoid hefty bank coin-counting fees and take advantage of the mint's no-fee reimbursements.

In order to close the loophole, new recommendations were handed down. Entities seeking reimbursement from the mint must now pack mutilated coins in smaller containers; include no more than a minimal number of machine-countable coins; and submit a Report of International Transportation of Currency or Monetary Instruments (FinCEN Form 105). (FinCEN stands for the Treasury's Financial Crimes Enforcement Network.) The law does not require redeemers to identify the source of their coins, and it is not technically illegal to submit unmutilated coins for redemption, but the mint rejects such submissions because only banks have the authority to redeem unmutilated coins. Additionally, mint employees now observe the reclamation process more closely and assay samples of all large shipments. As a spokesman put it, the mint program is "essentially a cash-for-cash redemption program that, if abused, could potentially be used as a mechanism for...fraud, tax evasion, and [violations of the] Bank Secrecy Act [the legislative act that requires financial institutions to work with government agencies to prevent money laundering]."[9] The feds, obviously, want none of that.

As much as money is governed by law, it is also subject to whim. The Mütter Museum at the College of Physicians of Philadelphia exhibits frighteningly altered coins in drawer after drawer of bezoars (masses found trapped in gastrointestinal systems). Humans aren't the only mammals who ingest money. Rats are known to line their nests with gnawed greenbacks, and in 2013 Dr. Cheryl Greenacre of the University of Tennessee College of Veterinary Medicine in Knoxville helped pull ninety-seven cents from a duck.[10] The law of nature means many birds are attracted to shiny, heavy things, and this duck, who lived in a teenager's bedroom, also had a necklace and earrings trapped in its esophagus. Greenacre does not know why children, dogs, and even alligators swallow indigestible objects, notably coins, but she says that nickels, dimes, and quarters aren't as much of a problem as modern pennies, the toxic zinc of which can lead to digestive and neurological problems.[11]

It is clear that serious wrongdoing with our almighty coins is a felony that can be vigilantly enforced. Then again, those guilty of minor infractions are sometimes let off the hook. In 1963 US marine Ronald Lee Foster of Beaver Falls, Pennsylvania, was fined twenty dollars and given one year of probation for "sweating" pennies by cutting off their rims and using them as dimes in the base's coin-operated laundry, cigarette, and soda machines. Half a century later, Foster was pardoned by President Barack Obama.

A HOLE IN YOUR POCKET

Intentionally Burned Money

Argumentum ad crumenam: The informal fallacy of concluding a statement is correct because the speaker is rich.

Argumentum ad lazarum: The informal fallacy of concluding a statement is incorrect because the speaker is poor.

BURNED MONEY IS A POTENT SYMBOL, as fraught with meaning as a battle-scarred flag. High rollers flaunt wealth by lighting cigars with hundred-dollar bills. Activists burn cash to register dissatisfaction. In 1996 the first online telerobotic lab opened, and visitors to its website could remotely operate a robot to engage in the illegal act of burning an actual hundred-dollar bill.[1] Fire-fused clumps of bills and coins from the 9/11 attacks are preserved for posterity in national museum collections. There are even occultists who carve magical symbols on coins and toss them into fire in the belief they will extinguish the flames.

It is illegal to burn or melt money but acceptable to turn it into art, jewelry, origami, or other creative goods. {Fig. 18} The US Mint does not promote coloring or otherwise altering US coinage, yet its website informs the public that "there are no sanctions against such activity absent fraudulent intent." The feds seem happy to reap the profit that arises from artistic production that takes coins out of circulation (meaning they will no longer be used as money ordinarily is) and gives them additional market value.

The earliest example I've found of an artwork depicting burned US money is *A Royal Flush*, a widely circulated and displayed 1899 print attributed to artist Charles Alfred Meurer. The print, featuring a realistic image of two

Fig. 18

Gay Merrill Gross invented this twenty-one-fold origami
model entitled *George Washington Framed*.

Confederate fifty-dollar notes—one newly minted atop another that is badly scorched—was understood at the time to suggest that the South would rise again. In 1927 Otis Kaye followed suit by making his political feelings public with *Money to Burn*, an oil-on-canvas painting depicting Civil War–era fractional currency (aka "paper coins"), a new ten-dollar bill, a spent matchstick, and a burned federal bill.

Eighty-three years later, contemporary artist Dread Scott used the same title for his live performance at the intersection of Broad and Wall Streets in Manhattan. One sunny June day in 2010, prefiguring Occupy Wall Street by more than a year, Scott came up from the subway wearing a shirt festooned with two hundred and fifty dollars in singles, fives, tens, and twenties. As deputy director of Franklin Furnace Archive, the nonprofit arts organization that funded his performance, I was on the scene. Carrying a bucket of sand and chanting "money to burn," Scott slowly marched to the front of the American Stock Exchange. He set down the bucket, plucked a bill from his shirt and a Zippo lighter from his pocket, and began setting the money afire. When the flame got close to his fingers, he snuffed it out and repeated the process. He invited passersby to join him with their own money, drawing curious looks and a small crowd. Some gaped, others reached into their billfolds. A wealthy woman I know asked for change for a five, so she could set just a single ablaze. Others scoffed and spat comments such as "Maybe you should just give it away," "Why don't you buy lunch for the homeless?" and "Those dollars could help cure cancer." These points were valid; I shared with their makers that, like many of us, the artist needed money and worked hard for his income. His higher aim, I continued, was to "highlight the profound polarization of wealth and income that exists" and to question our profit-based systems.[2] Scott's intention in burning money on Wall Street was to parallel destructive closed-door activities of banks and traders and to argue that humanity is better served when people take care of one another.

In preparation for *Money to Burn*, Scott and Franklin Furnace had worked with a prominent civil-rights attorney and other legal experts and came to understand that the only aspect of the performance that was against the law was the open flame. Thus, Scott's bucket of sand. I was nervous but confident that we were within the law and felt comfortable taking a position against the police barricades protecting the stock exchange. I was soon joined by a black-suited, pinkie-ringed investor who'd come out for a smoke. His ID tag read "Barb," and, true to his name, he began vehemently airing opinions: "That's illegal," "He should be arrested," and so on. I asked him which law made it illegal. He had no answer and continued his harangue: "Throw the bum in jail—money's the lifeblood of our nation." I tried once more to reason with him and asked if it were legal to burn the flag. When he replied, "Of course not," I realized my efforts to change this patriot's mind were futile.

A pair of policemen rounded the corner. They kept their distance and discussed the happening between themselves. They were soon joined by another and then another pair of cops. I sidled over when a more menacing patrolman came on the scene and got on his walkie-talkie. The first cop muttered to his partner, "Here we go—Hardball's got his panties in a knot again." Finally, the police moved in and asked Scott for identification, which he readily provided. Hardball said, "As far as I'm concerned you're being disorderly right now."

Scott surprised him. "I'm being disorderly?" he responded softly. "If you want me to stop, I can stop," and he did. Scott was issued a summons for disorderly conduct, and everyone went on their way. When the case came to court it was thrown out, as video evidence clearly recorded the artist obeying the police.[3]

Was Scott's act legal or not? The law prohibits intentional destruction of money but says we're allowed to use money to create works of art. Scott's intent was artistic, and there are many precedents for using fire to create art. The most prized ceramics in Japan, for example, are tea bowls with blackened surfaces created by the intense heat and smoke of the raku method of firing. Scott's work might have even helped create a new law about burning money, akin to that which protects flag burning as free speech. He knew what people would think about his piece, and he explains: "It's crazy to burn money on the street, but it is the height of rationality to have a market where billions of dollars can vanish on a bad day."[4] At least for now, as Scott's example shows, those seeking to make artistic or political statements by burning money are operating in a gray area between art and immolation, between fire's dual capacity to destroy and forge anew.[5]

HONEST WEAR

*The Discovery of an
Anticounterfeiting Secret*

WHEN I SAW HOW BEAUTIFULLY artist Cyrilla Mozenter wove faded and flaccid bills into her canvases, I began the hunt for a beat-up buck of my own. It wasn't long before I found my weathered wonder. {Fig.19} This 1999-series single had been circulating for only five years when I became its final owner. The verso (back side) is unremarkable, but I keep it because I love handling its fuzzy and faded recto (front side). The black ink has gone ashen. The engraved signatures are illegible. George Washington seems hidden behind a gauzy gray veil. "Just spend it already," people tell me, but I'm far too attached to the look and feel and stories engendered by well-worn and near-derelict cash.

Once, when I was idly staring at this bill, I realized it's not as faded as I'd assumed. Yes, most of the black ink is gone, but the black seal of the Federal Reserve Bank of San Francisco and its four corresponding numeral 12s are almost as dark as new. Why had only some of the black faded? Suddenly, my single seemed important. I continued my investigations.

Around that time, a tech-savvy friend invested in a company that was developing bar codes for currency and creating algorithms for unique sequencing to deter counterfeiting and money laundering. He gave me a Vistatector Magnetic Ink Detector 99X, a pen-sized battery-operated device for checking the authenticity of currency by verifying the presence of magnetic particles. I learned that only some of the black ink used to print US money contains this easy-to-detect magnetic oxide (I presume that this iron oxide powder destabilizes the ink, making it prone to fading). Bankers, retailers, couriers, hoteliers, and the like are privy to this information, but the public is not generally in the know about money's magnetic inks (and what must be a host of additional secret anticounterfeiting measures).

Fig. 19

Very worn one-dollar bill

Counterfeiting has been a problem since the invention of money. In the 1700s, for example, when British visitors saw the First Nations using seashells for currency, they began forging wampum out of porcelain (their counterfeits rarely succeeded). The US Secret Service was initially founded to stem counterfeiting. The agency remains "committed to zero tolerance and is determined to investigate each and every counterfeiting case."[1] Secret Service agents work on anti-counterfeiting with colleagues from the FBI, the Treasury, the Federal Reserve System, and regional and local authorities.

US currency is created on $7 million Super Orlof presses, which have 185,634 parts and exert up to 60 tons of pressure to force ink into bills. Ordinary presses merely layer ink on the surface of paper and cannot compete with this massive machine's power and fineness of line. It is the tactility imparted by such high-quality intaglio printing that, in part, gives our money its distinctive feel. It's why people can discern real bills from counterfeits by feel alone.

The Bureau of Engraving and Printing identifies the more than two-hundred-year-old Crane & Co. of Dalton, Massachusetts, as the original and exclusive maker of the 75 percent cotton and 25 percent linen bond used for US currency, but that's not the full story. Paper money is a misnomer—our bills are actually made of cloth. Linen is not necessarily a type of material; it is a type of weaving that can be done with silk, wool, or any other fiber. It is linen from the flax plant that gives US banknotes their distinctive "tooth" and enables them to survive rigorous durability tests involving repeated crumpling, folding, laundering, soiling, and soaking in solvents, acids, and gasoline. Coins last an average of thirty years, but one-dollar bills circulate for less than six. Fifties have the shortest life expectancy (3.7 years); hundreds, the world's most respected store of value, stay in circulation the longest (around 15 years). We take care of our Benjies.

When a Federal Reserve bank receives worn-out money from commercial banks, it performs a complex analysis of each note.[2] In the 1940s and '50s, it canceled bills using diamond-shaped punch-outs: two each, in the top and bottom halves of the worn bills. In the 1970s and '80s, before the implementation of toxic magnetic inks in the 1990s, shabby scrip was incinerated at the rate of 1.2 million pieces per day. Today, bills that are soiled, defaced, limp, torn, partially destroyed, disintegrated, or plumb worn out are given numerical grades from one to five and shredded.[3] Since 2012 these shreds have been sent to a farm in Delaware, which converts thirty tons of cash to compost per week. Even though we might not be aware of it, our money is in constant flux. The bills in our wallets are slowly eroding; thankfully, the US government's covert and overt vigilance in ensuring our trust is not.

The Bank Manager Who Throws Away a Grand a Year

...but I'm not bound and I never will
Be to a wrinkled crinkled wadded dollar bill.
"Wrinkled Crinkled Wadded Dollar Bill," 1968 song
written by Vince Matthews and sung by Johnny Cash

My best friend, Joe, has been a banker
for more than three decades. He started
as a teller in 1980 and now manages
a bank with more than $400 million in
assets. He's as honest as a summer day
is long and good at the work. He can,
for example, by feel alone, unfailingly
distinguish the denominations of US
currency.[4]

One autumn night in the mid-1980s
I called Joe to shoot the breeze.
"What's cooking?" I asked.

"Not much," he said. "The wife
and daughter are good; I'm making my
mortgage; and—oh, yeah—I threw out
$870.53 earlier tonight."

"Huh? Come again?" I inquired,
incredulous, of the guy I'd trusted to
divvy every tab we'd ever rung up.

"I just threw away almost a grand,"
Joe replied impassively.

"C'mon, man, stop pulling my leg."

"No, seriously, I threw out nine
hundred large tonight. Not only that,
my boss told me to."

"You gotta be kidding."

"Nope. I took a small cardboard box,
threw in a few hundred coins and bills,
taped it up well, said goodnight to the
staff, waited until everyone was gone,
turned on the alarm..."

"What hey?" I interrupted, realizing
he might be serious. "Forget the rest,
just tell me which Dumpster," I added
breathlessly. "I'll fly out tonight.
Dinner's on me."

"You know I can't do that, Harley.
So anyways, I locked the doors of the
bank, went out to the parking lot, shoved
my little box deep down in a Dumpster,
and drove home."

"You're not kidding?"

"No. It was part of my job. I do it
every year."

"You're really not kidding. What
gives?"

"Well, you know how some money gets
so mangled that only the banks will
accept it? You know what banks do with
those beat up coins and bills? We call
'em 'mutes,' and they're a pain in the
neck. For each piece of money that comes
in mutilated, we have to fill out federal
paperwork; label and bundle it according
to strict regulations; and return it,
insured, to the Bureau of Engraving
[bills] and the mint [coins]. Then we
wait for the government to take its
sweet time determining how much they'll
replace—sometimes up to a year. The time
it would take for my staff to prepare
the mutes and complete the forms and
monitor the progress would be extensive
and end up costing the bank more in
salary and overhead than the mutes are
worth. So, no, I can't tell you where,
but as part of my job, once a year, I
throw away about a thousand US dollars."

Hard as it may be to fathom, under
certain circumstances, banks save money
by throwing it away. If only things were
so easy for us ordinary Joes.

HAMILTON, FRANKLIN, BIV, JUROR, AND GOLDEN

Colorful Men of Money

ALEXANDER HAMILTON

Once I spotted a cozy-looking four-dollar pair of corduroys at the thrift store, so I tried them on, shoved my hand in a pocket, and struck a pose. "Eww," I thought, as I pulled out a square of cloth the same mossy green as the pants, "someone left his hankie." Into the wastepaper basket it went, but as it fluttered down, it unfolded, and Alexander Hamilton peered up through the murk. I snatched back the barely recognizable ten-dollar bill, paid for the pants, and pocketed the profit. My next thought—"Free lunch!"—was derailed when I realized if I spent the sawbuck, I'd never see another like it. This all took place a couple of decades ago, but I still remember checking the pockets one last time before giving the worn-out wide wales back to the thrift store where I scored this extragreen green. {Fig. 20}

I'm not the first to make note of stained banknotes. J. H. Griffith wrote on the topic in 1877 in *Money As It Was and Is*, spelling out the rules for exchanging worn money

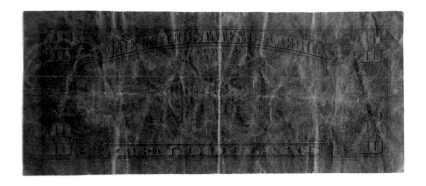

Fig. 20
The front of this ten-dollar bill is
slightly less stained.

73

and cataloging the ways banknotes could become mutilated through accidental contact with industrial oil, paint, and acid processes. These produced, he wrote, "strange results; instead of greenbacks, they are sometimes blackbacks, or partly or entirely blue, red or yellow—in fact all the colors which dyes can make them."[1]

TREY JUROR

People stain bills with differing degrees of intentionality. Sometimes bills get stained by accident (next time you buy a pint of wild berries from a forager, check the color of your change). {Fig. 21, third row, second column} Sometimes people doing dirty jobs don't have rags at hand and grab at anything absorbent. I don't know how most of the bills in my collection got their added colors, but I can explain the yellow one shown in the fourth row, second column of Fig. 21. In 1973 artist Paul McMahon was working in a gas station, making change all day, when he was struck by a funny idea: "What if people gave me regular money, and I gave them colored money as change?" He got some dye, stained fifteen bucks or so in the three primary colors, and had so much fun he still makes new editions from time to time. The one I have is countersigned with a classic McMahon pun, directly over the engraved signature of Henry M. Paulson Jr.: "Trey Juror."

BEN FRANKLIN

Why is US money green? No one knows for sure, but the Bureau of Engraving and Printing has some pretty good guesses. In general, the bureau tells us, green pigment is readily available in large quantities; is relatively higher in resistance than other colors to chemical and physical changes

Fig. 21
Except for the yellow bill I bought from artist
Paul McMahon, these one-dollar notes were acquired
in ordinary transactions.

like fading, flaking, and discoloration; and is psychologically identified with strength and stability. The particular green of US money originated around the same time as photography in the mid-1800s, when an increase in the fraudulent erasing and reprinting of bills with higher denominations called for special colored inks that could not be cleanly removed. One such ink, a green, earned a copyright—and star status as the main color of US currency. The innovative hue, still the primary color used on US bills, is known as "patent green."

Maybe the choice of green also relates to Benjamin Franklin's turn to nature for motifs that would help stem the counterfeiting that was rampant during the eighteenth century. Starting in 1739, Franklin printed banknotes with images of blackberry, willow, and other leaves that displayed complex shapes, unevenly serrated edges, and subtly gradated vein systems. Franklin's banknotes bore the frightful inscription: "To Counterfeit is DEATH"; when that did not deter criminals, careful comparisons of the leaf prints' singular shapes could uncover their deceptions. Franklin's leaf-print method was ingenious, but if it were truly as counterfeit-proof as the great inventor believed, we would not need the more colorful currency technologies in use today.

ROY G. BIV

Most of the world's national currencies use color coding to differentiate denominations. Not so the United States, producers of staid, mostly black-and-green banknotes from the get-go until 2003, when the Bureau of Engraving and Printing started issuing its most colorful bills to date.[2] About this use of color in the first completely redesigned bill in sixty-seven years, a Treasury spokesman said, "It is purely a security feature and something to aid the public. It isn't just something to make it pretty and different."[3] For centuries US banknotes were drab. Now they cover the spectrum with gradations and patterns in pastel shades of red, orange, yellow, green, blue, indigo, and violet (aka Roy G. Biv).

Current US banknotes worth ten dollars or more feature metallic, color-shifting inks as alluring as the silver-and-green shimmer of olive tree leaves. You can view these iridescent pigments by tilting one of the larger notes and watching the numerals in the lower right corner shift in color, similar to how custom-painted cars approach an observer in one color and change to another color as they motor away. My eye doctor explained how such double refractivity works and told me about a Costa Rican national park where thieves break in and steal birefringent vegetation. The authorities don't know why; it is our conjecture that the plant pilferers are in cahoots with counterfeiters.

Late twentieth- and early twenty-first-century bills contain ghostly watermarks and discreet polymer security ribbons that display fluorescent color when excited by ultraviolet light. {Fig. 22} When I first inspected these plastic ribbons under ultraviolet light, I worked my way up from the hot-blue five-dollar bill to the glowing-orange ten-dollar bill and grew more and more excited to see what surprises the hundred-dollar bill might have in store. Alas, it was a letdown. Its pinkish strip is not as bright as those of its fiscal inferiors. Figuring something was amiss, I returned again and again to the bank to exchange my bills for new samples, but the hundred's strips were always the palest. Might this be part of a counterintuitive approach to crime prevention? Just as it was easier to make strong glue than to develop Post-it

Fig. 22

One- and two-dollar notes do not have ultraviolet strips like other denominations of US bills. The 2013 hundred-dollar note (the second fluorescent strip from left) features a brighter pink strip than its predecessor (the far left strip).

Notes with adhesive that can be cleanly removed, bright fluorescents might be easier to formulate than faint ones.

The United States regularly upgrades its anticounterfeiting endeavors. Try scanning a twenty-first-century bill on your computer, and you won't get a reproduction—you'll get a stern Secret Service warning flashing on your monitor. Creating such smart technology takes time, and the first colorized hundred-dollar bill wasn't released until ten years after the first full-color bill, the twenty. The complex new Benjie took more than a decade to develop, and production costs are estimated at more than $100 million. Some of the expense arose from a theft of new hundreds a year before their official release date. Additionally, at least thirty million imperfect bills had to be destroyed. The newest hundreds, officially designated Series 2009A, weren't released to the public until mid-October 2013. Their hidden fluorescent strips are brighter pink than their predecessors', and they contain other newfangled features, including a copper-colored inkwell that, when tilted, causes a greenish-gold Liberty Bell to flicker. Most amazing of all are the blue security ribbons woven through the front of the bills. These quarter-inch-wide strips feature thousands of imperceptible microlenses that magnify microprinting and make dizzying 3-D Liberty Bells and numeral 100s whirl about. Seven months after the release of the new-generation hundred-dollar bills, in order to deter fraud and abuse of the currency redemption process, the Bureau of Engraving and Printing hastened the release of the first amended regulations on the exchange of mutilated bills since April 1991. You still need clearly more than 50 percent of a banknote to cash it in, but now bills submitted for redemption also depend on the Bureau of Engraving and Printing's determination of whether they contain "sufficient remnants of any relevant security feature."[4] There are other anti-counterfeiting technologies hidden within our money—but on this subject the feds are mum.

SAM GOLDEN

The self-described color junkies of Golden Artist Colors of New Berlin, New York, the specialty artists' paint manufacturing business begun by Sam Golden in 1980,[5] introduced a new line of paint the next year.[6] Known as Panspectra, these bright metallic paints, when tilted, covered nearly the entire spectrum of visible light. The active ingredient was magnesium fluoride, a rare colorless-to-white mineral with intensely prismatic crystals. The dramatic pigment came with a hefty price tag (nearly one hundred times that of standard paint powders), but any bottle that might remain today could command an even higher price—a few years after the introduction of Panspectra, Golden acceded to a federal request to cease production. Presumably the US government was concerned that Golden's product could be used to simulate aspects of its new bills.

Concerns about security and profit motivate government treasuries to continually revise coins and bills. The US government has issued only coins with natural metal tones, but radiant hand-colored coins sometimes appear in pocket change, most often the glossy red "house quarters" that establishments give out so customers can play jukeboxes, pool, pinball, and video games for free. This marked-quarters gimmick not only attracts customers, it helps keep them from spending the free money on their bar tab. {Fig. 23, four corners} Others profit by colorizing coins, most notably the Royal Canadian Mint, which in 2010 released a twenty-dollar silver coin embedded with purple Swarovski crystals. Maybe someday the US Mint will follow the Bureau of Engraving and Printing's example and, like Canada, enliven its palette.

US government websites are surprisingly transparent about moneymaking technologies—they want the public to know how to protect itself—but less revealing about the success of their crime-prevention strategies. One wonders about the effectiveness of the elaborate new colors and proprietary inks. Do particolored bills have unintended negative effects, such as making high-denomination money easier to spot and steal? Do people with low vision need higher-relief engravings to distinguish the denominations, or are they better served by the addition of large, colored numerals or by denomination-identifying apps like the BEP's EyeNote? Does adding color to US currency make things more difficult for forgers, or will improvements in scanning technology render colorization ineffectual? Will the pot of gold at the end of the Treasury's rainbow, a counterfeit-proof currency, ever be realized? Color me skeptical.

Fig. 23
Found colorful quarters

FROGSKINS AND CARTWHEELS

Nicknames for Money

MONEY IS A HUMAN INVENTION. It gleams as it decays, singing its siren song 24-7-365. As money is many things to many people, it goes by many names. Whether banker or gangster, spender or saver, everyone uses $lang. I love collecting $obriquets—the funnier, coarser, and more affectionate, far-fetched, and born of secrecy, the better.

Here's my running list:

A
Abe
Abraham
Ag
Au

B
bacon
bank
banknote
bankroll
batter
beans
Benjamin
Benjie
berries
big one
bill
bit
black eagle
blueback
bob
Bolivars

bones
boodle
bottom dollar
bread
bread and honey
breeches
buck
buckaroo
bullion
buzzard dollar

C
C-note
cabbage
cake
capital
cartwheel
cash
CF
chalupas
cheddar
cheddar cheese
cheese

chicken fat
chicken feed
chicken scratch
chinchilla
ching ching
chink
chump change
chunky
cizzash
clams
cold hard cash
collards
commas
copper
cream
cream cheese

D
dead presidents
dibs
dime
dinar
dinero

do-it
dolluh
dolo
double eagle
dough
dub
ducat
dust

F
farthing
fetti
fin
five spot
fiver
flash note
folding money
folding stuff
FRN
frogskins

G
G
G-stacks
get
gold
good sum
Gouda
grand
gravy
green
green stuff
greenback

groat
Gucci
guinea
gwop
gwopington

H
half sawbuck
half a rock
horse blanket
hundo
hundy
hunnert

I
ingot

J
jack
Jackson

K
K
ka-ching
kale
kite
kitty

L
lana
large
lettuce
lolly

long bit
long green
loot
lucci
lucre
lump sum

M
M
mad stacks
mazuma
mint
mite
moolah
mooney
mopus
moss

N
nickel
nickel note
note
nuff-nuff
nugget

O
orange peel

P
paper
pelf
penny
peso

phony baloney
pile
plata
plug nickel
plum
pocket
pound
proceeds
purse

R
ready
receipts
red
red cent
rent
rhino
rice
riches
Roanoke
rock
roll
rouleau
round sum
rutabaga

S
salt
sawbuck
scoots
scratch
scrilla
scroll

seawant
shekel
shells
shinplaster
short bit
silver
simoleon
sinews of war
sister
skins
slip
slug
smacker
smackeroo
smacks
sou
sourdough
specie
spondoolies
spondulicks
spreadalotta
stacks
sterling
stiver
sum
sum total

T
ten spot
tenner
tester
thundo
tin

toadskins
treasure

V
V
vee

W
wad
wagon wheel
wampum
watermelon
wealth
wherewithal
wonga

Y
yaper
yard
yayber
yen

ILLUSTRATED TAXONOMY

and Glossary of Mutilated Money

PEOPLE OF ALL TYPES participate in the mutilation of money: warriors and lovers, hoboes and bankers, police and vandals alike. Whether intentionally or by the tiniest of changes we unconsciously cause by handling bills and coins, we all alter money.

The most egregious mutilators of money are governments. In 31 CE, when Sejanus (soldier and advisor to the Roman emperor Tiberius) failed to overthrow Tiberius, he was not only executed, he was caused to suffer *damnatio memoriae*. This meant that, among other punishments, the government obliterated his name from coins that had been created in his honor and continued to circulate them. Since at least the seventeenth century, governments have recalibrated bills and adjusted the weight of coins to meet fluctuating standards. Instead of paying for expensive new engravings every time change is necessitated by inflation or politics, for example, governments may create "new" currency by re-engraving existing money.

The US Mint's coin production numbers mirror my own holdings: a preponderance of pennies, followed by quarters, nickels, and then dimes.[1] {**Figs. 23, 24, 25; also see front and back covers, page 10**} I have only three marred dollar coins, and, until recently, had no seriously worn half dollars. So it was exciting to learn that in 2003 the mint started using Dutch "waffling" machines to crush defective brand-new coins, thus canceling their monetary value. Since the crushed coins are no longer legal tender, this in-house demolition eliminates the need for mint police to escort rejected coinage to the private vendors who melt and recycle US coin metal. When I learned that the mint does not object to the trade of these former coins, because they have been paid for by the vendors

Fig. 24

Ten pretty, mutilated nickels

Fig. 25

Twenty-one exquisitely ugly dimes

Fig. 26

A John F. Kennedy half dollar
intentionally mutilated by the US Mint (left).
Standard Kennedy half (right).

and the waffled discs are no longer considered US government property, I bought a crumpled Kennedy half dollar from
Waffle Coins Inc. of Bridgewater, New Jersey, to fill the gap in
my collection.[2] {Fig. 26} It is the only mutilated coin for which
I have paid more than face value. I love it because of the strik-
ing damage done by the mint, and because even though the
coin is beyond repair, it comes with an official numismatic
grade of "brilliant uncirculated."

Money goes everywhere and can react with any and
all substances on earth, whether intentionally, erroneously,
or naturally. Cash can be ruined by forces of nature or by
machines of any description. The damage, whether benign or
pernicious, can range from minor to severe, from common to
unprecedented. Sometimes money is even mutilated for practical purposes: authenticators of coins must sometimes use
invasive methods.

I once saw an elderly man bent over the middle of
Fifty-Sixth Street in Woodside, Queens, so I asked if he was
OK. He pointed to his nearby apartment and explained, "I'm
wedging in a nickel to stop the damn sewer cap from clanging
every time a car rolls by." I returned a few days later to check;
the sewer cap was snugly in place and the noiseproofing
nickel had disappeared. Beyond such practical, nonfiscal use,
money is also deployed for aesthetic, experimental, fraudulent, symbolic, and other purposes, as noted in the following
glossary of causes of money mutilation not covered elsewhere
in this book:

Accessories: Coins can be altered and incorporated as design features of belts, purses, et cetera.

Advertising: Despite federal law prohibiting advertising via writing, printing, or otherwise impressing upon or attaching materials to coins and currency, there are more than 13,500 known types of merchant-countermarked coins (coins to which corporate names and advertising have been added).[3] Various modern methods exist for marking banknotes, such as the use of adhesive labels. It is natural for companies to capitalize on the fact that money circulates widely. {Figs. 27, 28}

Fig. 27	Fig. 28
This 1840 Braided Hair Large Cent bears the merchant countermarks "L. Coon" on the front and "Abbott" on the back.	The theme of the three-part 2004 miniseries advertised on this one-dollar bill was illegal global trafficking.

Aerugo: The rust of metal, especially brass or copper. Also known as verdigris.

Armor: Even after a government has gone belly-up and its coins no longer have fiscal value, the solid discs of metal can be pierced, strung, and worn by warriors as chain mail. This has been a common practice in Croatia and parts of the Arab world.

Bag toning: Bright rainbow colors on an otherwise pristine coin, created when coins are pressed for a long time against the sulfurous material used in certain cloth coin bags.

Bar tricks: Drinkers like to make bets on questions like whether it's possible to cut a banknote (still in one piece) in such a way that a person can step through the resulting hole. (It can be done.)

Batteries: Coins made of various metals can be sandwiched between saltwater-laden pads to make electric batteries.

Blistering: Welder's torches are sometimes used to create strange surfaces on coins, which may be polished to make the distortions look like mint errors.

Carbon spotting: Brown to black oxidation marks.

Chop mark: A small, rubber-stamped symbol on currency made by international bankers or money exchangers to indicate that they have examined and found a bill genuine. This can eliminate duplicating verification efforts and is equivalent to a countermark on a coin. Most often found on large-denomination bills.[4] {**Fig. 29**}

Fig. 29

Two rubber-stamped chop marks of unknown meaning on a twenty-dollar bill

Cleaning: The most common cause of banknote rejection by federal authorities is soiling. The primary source of soiling is human grease, known as sebum, which collects on bills as they pass from person to person. Rhode Island scientists Nabil M. Lawandy and Andrei Y. Smuk created a banknote washing chamber using the gas and liquid properties of supercritical carbon dioxide to clean bills without harming security features.[5] The technique mitigates the spread of disease by removing organism colonies such as bacteria and could reduce central bank budgets for banknote replacement and also lessen the environmental impact of discarding unfit banknotes.

Contamination: Money exposed to or damaged by contaminants may emit offensive odors and pose health hazards and safety risks. Those seeking reimbursement must submit contaminated money in doubled autoclave bags akin to those used in medical sterilization machines. In cases of natural disasters, banks will often provide bags with moisture and oxygen barriers designed to provide leak and odor protection. Money exposed to any biological or chemical "bioterrorist agent" is handled separately by the Federal Reserve.

Counterfeit coins: Primarily to simulate rare coins, criminals make fakes with sand, clay, metal, and lost-wax casting processes and by altering genuine coins. While not always involving physical mutilation, counterfeiting can be seen as a form of philosophical mutilation in that the illegal practice can erode confidence and trust in currency.

Countermark: Governmental or nongovernmental stamping on a coin. Countermarks, also known as overstamps, are found on almost all silver coins of the Sultanates that circulated in Bengal from the thirteenth through the sixteenth centuries. These were frequently revalued by currency traders and exchange brokers of the period, who used three basic types of countermarks to indicate they had vetted the coin in question: (1) marks made by small, light punches bearing graphic designs; (2) large, deep cancellation marks gouged by chisel; and (3) shallow, round holes made by testers.[6]

Cud: Numismatic term for an imperfection (usually a blob raised above the edge of a coin) caused by a crack, chip, or other damage to a coin-making die.

Debased: Having below-standard metal content.

Drawing: Banknotes are frequently tallied or doodled on or used for scratch paper. {**Fig. 30**} For an extensive collection of such alterations, see http://www.johnnyburrito.com/uglymoney.htm and http://www.memolition.com/2013/10/20/turning-money-into-art-19-pictures/.

Fig. 30
Several people added graffiti to
this one-dollar bill.

Dropping: Coins can be intentionally or accidentally dropped from tall buildings or into storm drains, sewage systems, wishing wells, et cetera. Experts can spot the resultant bumps on coin rims.

Elongated cents: Souvenirs made by placing a cent in a machine that flattens coins into ovals and embosses them with keepsake information. First introduced at the World's Columbian Exposition in Chicago in 1893. Dimes can also be elongated in these machines.

Fig. 31
The red rubber-stamping on this bill reads "EVIDENCE:
IF PRESENTED NOTIFY N.Y.C. POLICE DEPT."

Embedding: Coins can be embedded in Lucite or other materials for display purposes.

Evidence: Money associated with a crime can be so marked by the authorities. {**Fig. 31**}

Exonumia: Items akin to money, such as medals, scrip, tokens, wooden nickels, et cetera.

FIDO: An obsolete numismatic acronym for Freaks, Imperfections, Defects, and Oddities (i.e., "dogs").

Folding: It takes four thousand double folds (forward and back) before a banknote begins to tear.

Food: Food or drink on money can cause decay and/or attract vermin.

Fusing: More than one coin or parts of coins may become stuck together, either in the minting process or with tar, glue, et cetera. Schemers have been known to intentionally laminate, glue, or otherwise brutalize and then intermingle real and fake banknotes to submit for redemption.

Garbage: Money can be accidentally discarded. According to May 2014 federal regulations, "No relief will be granted on account of lawfully held paper currency which has been totally destroyed.[7]

Gutter: Money can be trapped in silt- and debris-laden running water.

Hobo nickels: Sculptures that creatively turn coins into miniature bas-reliefs of skulls, cartoon characters, et cetera. The nickel's size, thickness, and relative softness make it a favored coin for such alterations.[8]

Jewelry: Coins can be looped, chained, engraved, enameled, turned into amulets, et cetera.

Laundry: Coin-operated washing machines can mangle coins trapped in their water pumps.

Fig. 32
Mutilated coin look-alikes
and one real coin. When
I spotted the authentic
and heavily damaged beauty
sitting underneath a
small foreign coin on the
exterior ledge of a cash
register at the Mulberry
Meat Market in Manhattan's
Chinatown, I offered to
buy it for face value.
The cashier, befuddled by
my request, was at first
silent. Then she smirked
and asked $10 for it.
I stood firm. She checked
with a colleague, got
the OK, and a trade was
effected for face value.

Fig. 33
The US Bureau of
Engraving sells
uncut sheets of
currency, with
which magicians and
others can make
props like this.

Look-alikes: Objects such as a blob of chewing gum (particularly cinnamon gum), round of foil (particularly from tubes of mints), washer, or switch-box punch-out can be mistaken for a coin (even by my five-year-old, who has twenty-twenty vision). {**Fig. 32**}

Love tokens: Nineteenth-century art pieces made by smoothing out and engraving coins with ornate monograms and romantic imagery. Men typically had these made at country fairs for their girlfriends.

Lucky money: People write notes on gift money, and businesses prominently display money inscribed by friends and colleagues.

Magic money: Magicians alter coins and bills to wow audiences. {**Fig. 33**}

Melting: Fluctuations in the international metal markets means that the worth of a coin's metal(s) can exceed its face value. One wealthy Texas investor is stockpiling twenty million nickels ($1 million). At the time of his purchase, the metal each nickel is made out of was worth 6.8 cents, but US Mint regulations forbid melting coins, so will he ever be able to legally capitalize on this differential? It is also illegal to carry certain amounts of particular coins out of the United States, and you can be jailed, for instance, if customs agents find you have ulterior motives for crossing international borders with as little as five dollars in pennies and nickels!

Natural forces: Geological and meteorological forces such as fire, earthquakes, floods, tornadoes, and hurricanes can wreak havoc with money, as can the slow and steady forces of wind, water, sand, and time.[9] These two Hurricane Sandy–flooded quarters come from rolls of change that were drying out over the toaster at Beach Bagel on 129th Street in Rockaway Park, New York, on its first day open after the storm. {**Fig. 34**}

Fig. 34
Two quarters salvaged from Hurricane Sandy
floodwaters, the Rockaway Peninsula, New York,
November 28, 2012

Fig. 35
Souvenir of the 1964-65 New York World's Fair:
a neutron-irradiated dime from the
Atomic Energy Commission's *Atomsville, U.S.A.*,
a children's exhibit about nuclear energy

Neutron irradiation: Several varieties of irradiated coins have been produced as novelty souvenirs over the years. One such souvenir came from the 1964–65 World's Fair at Flushing Meadows Corona Park in Queens, New York. {**Fig. 35**}

Novelties: Money can be turned into lucky charms, coins in a bottle, et cetera. Coins can also be hollowed out and made into secret capsules.

Organic substances: Acids, bacteria, bodily excretions and secretions, chemicals, chlorine, dampness, dirt, dyes, grease, gum, humidity, iron oxide, iron sulfide, mold, oil, rust, salt, sap, smoke, soil, soot, tar, and water can damage money. Numismatists are careful when talking around collectible money, as saliva can be corrosive.

Perfins: Punched perforated initials. {see **Fig. 31**}

Piercing: (also known as holing). Pierced coins are popular jewelry adornments. Hoodoo practitioners puncture silver dimes—to wear them around the neck or ankle as talismans. In related traditions, sigils (magic signs) are written on currency to turn it into "trained hunting money." In a dentistry district in Kathmandu, Nepal, people hoping for painless treatment nail coins into *Vaisha Dev*, the Toothache Tree. This orange plastic–spiked penny was nail-gunned into a concrete floor in performance artist Rumiko Tsuda's 1988 *Art Ceremony*. {**Fig. 36**}

Fig. 36
Making jewelry seems to be the primary
reason people pierce coins.

Plugging: Filling in a hole in a coin with metal. A coin with a filled hole or holes is called a plug. This is the origin of the expression "not worth a plug nickel."

Pop-outs: Coins with high-relief portraits that rise well above their rims were a patented invention introduced at the 1904 World's Fair in St. Louis and promoted again in the 1960s.

Potty coins: It was common for nineteenth-century jokers to carve images of toilets into coins bearing the image of a seated Lady Liberty.

Punching: See *perfins*.

RTM: An acronym for "return to me," sometimes seen on currency.

Rubber-stamping: One of the most common ways to use currency as a messenger is to rubber-stamp banknotes. This inexpensive means of publishing can reach a broad public. One often-spotted rubber-stamping directs people to the crowd-sourced bill-tracking website http://www.wheresgeorge.com.

Shrinking: The cloth used to make US banknotes can be shrunk. Artists using a proprietary heat and water process created a bill I purchased at the Whitney Museum of American Art gift shop in 1997. {**Fig. 37**} The shrunken single is thicker and stiffer than standard dollars, but, like all US banknotes, it still weighs exactly one gram. Alas, I failed to record the artists' names, and the Whitney's archive has no information. Coins can also be shrunk via elaborate processes; see http://www.capturedlightning.com/frames/shrinkergallery.html.

Fig. 37
When shrunk, this one-dollar note
became thicker than a standard dollar.

Fig. 38
Silk-screened quarters are a less-
common alternative to baseball cards.
©Merrickmint.com

Fig. 39
Beautifully smoothed nickel found in pocket
change by the artist Dolores Zorreguieta

Fig. 40
My seventh-grade shop-class experiment

Silk-screening: Messages and images can be silk-screen printed onto money. {**Fig. 38**}

Smoothing: Age, use, and abuse can all conspire to smooth out a coin's relief. {**Fig. 39**}

Soldering: This scarred, solder-splattered penny is one of only four or five coins I have intentionally mutilated. {**Fig. 40**} In seventh-grade shop class I experimented with tin snips but could not cut through this penny and eventually melted solder onto it. The others were hacksawed roughly in half so I could inspect their interiors.

Specimen bills: The word *specimen* is stamped vertically in red capital letters on examples of banknotes the Federal Reserve sends as reference tools to banks around the world. Specimen bills are not legal tender.

Spooned edges: Sailors were known to while away time by hammering with the heel of a spoon on the edge of a coin to thicken it. They would then hollow out the centers of the coins and fashion rings for missed loved ones.

Stitching: People use a variety of methods to rejoin torn and heavily-worn bills. Clear tape is used a lot today but when Ben Franklin–designed banknotes were circulating people added cloth or paper backings and/or sewed the bills back together. Several such repaired banknotes are on display at the Newman Money Museum at Washington University in St. Louis, Missouri.

Street scraping: Coins can have strata exposed or be otherwise damaged when dragged along streets by motor vehicles. {**Fig. 41**}

Stretching: I have never seen a stretched bill but presume someone knows how to elongate banknotes. See *elongated cents*.

Submersion: Coral, crystals, and rust can grow on coins that have been submerged underwater.[10] Bronze, copper, nickel, and zinc coins can be destroyed in ocean waters, as can banknotes, but silver and gold coins can survive encrustation and concretions mostly unscathed if they are of high enough fineness.

Swallowing: Money retrieved from the body cavities of people or animals (live or dead) is often found to be mutilated; blood, urine, feces, and other bodily matter can also damage money.

Synthetic materials: Adhesives, bleach, chewing gum, dye, gasoline, glue, ink, metal plating, oil, paint, stickers, tape, et cetera, can alter money.

Variety collectors: A subset of numismatists specializing in the minute details that differentiate what most people see as ordinary multiples.

Self-identified variety collectors specialize in coins that leave the mint with mistakes or anomalies such as off-center imagery or matte finishes (which are supposed to be reserved for specimen coins only). Several groups of variety collectors have banded together to form a society called the Combined Organizations of Numismatic Error Collectors of America. The group's website features a fiendishly detailed online glossary of terms such as "spiked heads" (when a cracked die leaves a ragged line through the head of a portrait bust on a coin); "pileups" (when coins get caught in the mint's machinery and fuse together); and "die clashes" (when the die for one side of the coin strikes so hard it leaves an impression on the other side). Variety experts can even identify tiny impressions such as those made by infinitesimal pieces of lint residue from the cloths used to polish coin-making dies.

Vegas coins: A nickname for coins heavily worn by use in slot machines.

Virtual currency: Bitcoin, Krugercoin, Megacoin, Peercoin, Zeuscoin, and other cryptocurrencies can be digitally mutilated. The physical tokens of such peer-to-peer digital currencies are subject to any real-world mutilation possibilities.

Fig. 41

The various insults and injuries, striations, nicks,
cuts, dents, and scratches these coins bear indicate
they were dragged along pavement by motor vehicles.
The cladding on the lower half of the quarter at the
bottom has been entirely scuffed off.

Notes

INTRODUCTION

1. Michael S. Shutty Jr., *One Coin Is Never Enough: Why and How We Collect* (Iola, WI: Krause Publications, 2011), 84.

2. Charles E. Anthon, *American Journal of Numismatics and Bulletin of the American Numismatic and Archaeological Society II* (June 1867): 3.

3. Jules David Prown, "Mind in Matter: An Introduction to Material Culture Theory and Method," *Winterthur Portfolio 17*, no. 1 (Spring 1982): 1.

4. Unless otherwise specified, all money and authorities discussed in this book are from the United States of America.

5. Mark Wagner, email to author, August 14, 2013.

UP LIKE A BAD PENNY

1. Clarence H. Vanselow and Sherri R. Forrester, "Shell Thickness of the Copper-Clad Cent," *Journal of Chemical Education* 70 (1993): 1023. The proportion of different metals used in coin making varies from year to year, but in general, of current US coins, cents have the least amount of copper (2.5 percent). Nickels are made of 75 percent copper; dimes, quarters, and halves of 91.67 percent copper; and Susan B. Anthony dollars of 87.5 percent copper.

2. Many of these early uses of copper cents were collected by Jason Goodwin in his book *Greenback: The Almighty Dollar and the Invention of America* (New York: Macmillan, 2003), 126–27.

3. David Margolick's paean to pennies ("Penny Foolish," *New York Times*, February 11, 2007) details the sensation: "The *Washington Star* compared the hordes outside the Mint there to the crowds watching the Wright brothers test their 'aeroplanes.'" Putting Lincoln's portrait on the penny, Margolick concludes, "was a revolutionary act: Up to then, the only figures on everyday American coins were allegorical figures, like Liberty. Putting real people on them, the thinking went, smacked of monarchy; even George Washington hadn't rated such treatment. To place Lincoln on the most widely circulated coin made sense; it was Lincoln, after all, who'd said that 'Common-looking people are the best in the world; that is the reason the Lord makes so many of them.'"

4. Including a counter-stamped 1840 cent (see Figure 27).

5. William H. Sheldon, MD, with the collaboration of Dorothy I. Pascal and Walter Breen, *Penny Whimsy: A Revision of Early American Cents, 1793–1814: An Exercise in Descriptive Classification with Tables of Rarity and Value* (New York: Harper and Brothers, 1958), 6.

6. An organization called Americans for Common Cents (http://www.pennies.org/) advocates for the penny.

7. Website of the United States Mint, http://www.usmint.gov/about_the_mint/fun_facts/?action=fun_facts10.

8. If, when you insert a penny headfirst into an automobile tire tread, the groove does not cover any portion of Lincoln's head, which is one-sixteenth of an inch from the rim, the tire lacks the requisite traction for safe driving.

SNEAK THIEVES

1. Sir John Craig, *Newton at the Mint* (Cambridge, UK: Cambridge University Press, 1946), 112.
2. It is easier to spot clipping and shaving if the coins are round to begin with. I asked Michael Pfefferkorn, a builder of several numismatic libraries, what I thought was a simple question: "Who made the first truly round coins?" His reply was staggering: "The problem lies in establishing a definition for the word *round*. If you examine the Aes Grave (third-century BCE cast bronze) coinage of Rome and the second-century BCE cast Chinese coinage, you will find round coins. The same can be said for fourth-century CE Roman copper, medieval English, Scottish, French, Italian, and others. Admittedly, some coins were badly struck and, as a result, have split or broadened edges. You need to consult [John S.] Davenport's series of books on German thalers. Another problem is the Hapsburg use of roller dies for mass production, which caused curvature and elongation of otherwise round planchets [pieces of metal readied for stamping into coins]. This is particularly noticeable in lower-denomination silver coins. I believe what you're looking for is absolute symmetry. Milled coinage (reeded edges) was indeed developed by Isaac Newton. There are several different kinds of edge modifications of which you should be aware. These include the normal reeded-edge coins we use today, the tulip edge [designs resembling tulips used to deter clipping] on Spanish Colonial silver after the demise of cob coinage [coins

hastily cut from bars of metal, resulting in more irregular coins than those made with planchets], and the lettered edge [coins] used in France and Italy. One way to approach this is to do it backwards. That is to say, instead of measuring for symmetry, measure for asymmetry. You then need to examine methods of manufacture for the coins in your study. Be careful not to overreach or you will finish your research in 3013! For the average person to understand what you are doing, you need to be mathematically clear in your determination of what is round and what is not, with the understanding that we see shapes in visual form but not mathematical form." Michael Pfefferkorn, email to author, September 13, 2013.
3. Peter Ackroyd, *Newton* (New York: Nan A. Talese, 2008), ebook, chap. 13.
4. "The Star and the Black Hole," *The Numismatist* (June 2001): 647–48.

FINE LINE

1. Alfred Frankenstein, *After the Hunt: William Harnett and Other American Still Life Painters, 1870–1900* (Berkeley: University of California Press, 1969), 82. For other early examples of paintings of money, see the essay by Bruce W. Chambers in *Old Money: American Trompe l'Oeil Images of Currency* (New York: Berry-Hill Galleries, 1988).
2. Ellen Wardwell Lee, Anne Robinson, and Alexandra Bonfante-Warren, *Indianapolis Museum of Art: Highlights of the Collection* (Indianapolis: Indianapolis Museum of Art, 2005), 138.
3. Frankenstein, *After the Hunt,* 151.
4. Mark Wagner, "Why Money?" in exhibition catalog *Money, Power, Sex & Mark Wagner* (New York: Pavel Zoubok Gallery, 2013), 15.

5. Ibid., 17. A video of currency collage artist Mark Wagner at work is online at http://www.vimeo.com/79148964 (accessed July 15, 2014).

6. Posting by Adamandia Kapsalais on Facebook, January 22, 2011, accessed July 2, 2014, https://www.facebook .com/adamandia.kapsalis/media _set?set=a.1382079108540.2047440 .1128831708&type=1&comment_id =837354&offset=0&total_comments=40.

7. It is legal for the public to make local banknotes (such as Ithaca Hours and Berkshire Bucks), but minting metal coins is forbidden. See Bernard von NotHaus's Liberty Dollars: http://www.fbi.gov /charlotte/press-releases/2011/defendant -convicted-of-minting-his-own-currency. The origins of the piggy bank are probably related to the medieval English word *pygg*, the term for clay used in the Middle Ages.

8. As stated in the certificate of authenticity accompanying the artwork, dated February 1, 2003, New York, New York, and signed by the artist and a gallery representative.

9. Gülşen Çalık, email to author, August 16, 2013.

CASE NO. 6-02848

1. "Titus, son of the Roman emperor Vespasian, had criticized a tax on public lavatories. Vespasian held a coin from the first payment to his son's nose and asked whether the smell was offensive. Titus said no. Vespasian replied, 'And yet it comes from urine' (Suetonius, *Vespasian* xxiii)." John Simpson and Jennifer Speake, eds., *The Oxford Dictionary of Proverbs*, 5th ed. (Oxford, UK: Oxford University Press, 2009), online edition.

2. Lydia Washington (public affairs specialist, BEP Office of External Relations), email to author, August 8, 2013.

3. Del Quentin Wilber, "Ruined U.S. Cash Worth Millions, but Stories are Priceless," *Washington Post*, October 5, 2009.

4. Opus 129, G major. The title for this piece may have been provided by Beethoven's friend Anton Schindler.

5. Department of the Treasury, letter to author, March 7, 1996.

6. Redeeming damaged money in the nineteenth century must have been a tricky task. Here's just a snippet of the 1877 Treasury regulations: "Entire pieces, constituting half or more than half, but less than three-fifths of notes, will be redeemed for but half of the full face value of the notes, except when accompanied by an affidavit made in conformity to paragraph 1." Today's terms are significantly more refined.

7. Department of the Treasury, letter to author, March 7, 1996.

8. Lydia Washington, email to author, October 7, 2013.

9. Paul Gilkes, "Mint adopts Mutilated Coin Redemption Program changes," *Coin World*, September 16, 2011, accessed July 3, 2014, http://www.coinworld.com/numismatic /coins/us-modern/mint-adopts-mutilated -coin-redemption-program.html.

10. Jon Kamp, "Chicken Owners Scramble When Their Pet Feels Foul: Craze of Raising Birds Grows, but Vets Are Scarcer Than Hen's Teeth," *Wall Street Journal*, September 23, 2013, and Dr. Cheryl Greenacre, interview by author, November 2013.

11. Website of National Center for Biotechnology Information, W. Rebhandl, A. Milassin, L. Brunner, I. Steffan, T. Benkö, M. Hörmann, J. Burtscher, "In vitro study of ingested coins: leave them or retrieve them?" Abstract. http://www.ncbi.nlm.nih .gov/pubmed/?term=zinc+swallowed +coins.

A HOLE IN YOUR POCKET

1. Legal Tender, accessed June 22, 2014, http://goldberg.berkeley.edu/art/tender/tender.html.

2. Dread Scott, artist's handout for *Money to Burn*, 2010.

3. Website of Dread Scott, *Money to Burn*, 2010, http://www.dreadscott.net/artwork/performance/money-to-burn.

4. Scott, handout, 2010. On August 15, 1971, President Richard M. Nixon took the nation off the gold standard, and US currency became fiat (meaning an arbitrary order from an authority, from the Latin for "let it be done"). Mathematical certainty be damned—the value of today's dollar is established by government decree and confirmed by our faith in Uncle Sam and every other person with whom we do business. Monetary systems are a human invention, an imprecise social science. Ultimately, even with mottoes such as "In God We Trust," money only works when people trust one another.

5. Urban legend has it that real money burns bright orange and counterfeit bills burn blue, but the near-constant upgrades in real bills and the great variety of counterfeits make me distrust that blanket belief.

HONEST WEAR

1. Website of the United States Secret Service, "Know Your Money," accessed August 5, 2014, http://www.secretservice.gov/money_technologies.shtml.

2. For example, "limpness is measured in automated sorting environments using acoustics and ultrasonic reflection," according to Nabil M. Lawandy and Andrei Y. Smuk, "Supercritical Fluid Cleaning of Banknotes," *Industrial and Engineering Chemistry Research* 53 (January 15, 2014): I.

3. According to the Federal Reserve System, approximately five billion unfit notes per year are destroyed at its East Rutherford Operations Center in New Jersey. In 2013 that amounted to $42 billion (statistics from the Museum of American Finance's 2013–14 exhibition *The Fed at 100*).

4. The international anticounterfeiting expert Yoshihide Matsumura of Matsumura Technology Co., Ltd., in Tokyo, Japan, is nicknamed "Golden Fingers" because he can, while blindfolded, distinguish authentic currency from counterfeits. Matsumura has exposed counterfeiting operations that make US one-hundred-dollar banknotes with engraving that is, tellingly, sharper than that of authentic bills.

HAMILTON, FRANKLIN, JUROR, AND GOLDEN

1. J. H. Griffith, *Money As It Was and Is* (New York: Eagle Job and Book Printing Department, 1877), 18.

2. US banknotes also feature tiny, evenly dispersed red and blue fibers and have included red, blue, and gold seals from time to time.

3. Bankrate, Jay MacDonald, "A rainbow of US money to appear in 2003," June 20, 2002, http://www.bankrate.com/brm/news/sav/20020420a.asp.

4. Federal Register, https://www.federalregister.gov/articles/2014/05/29/2014-12435/exchange-of -mutilated-paper -currency, accessed August 21, 2014.

5. Website of Golden Artist Colors, "A History of GOLDEN Artist Colors, Inc.," accessed June 23, 2014, http://www.goldenpaints.com/company/history.php.

6. Website of Golden Artist Colors, *Just Paint*, October 2001, accessed July 1, 2014, http://www.goldenpaints.com/justpaint/jp7article4.php.

gests these steps for redeeming flood-fire-damaged money:

(a) Regardless of the condition of the currency, do not disturb the fragments any more than is absolutely necessary.

(b) If the currency is brittle or inclined to fall apart, pack it carefully in plastic and cotton without disturbing the fragments and place the package in a secure container.

(c) If the currency was mutilated in a purse, box, or other container, it should be left in the container to protect the fragments from further damage.

(d) If it is absolutely necessary to remove the fragments from the container, send the container along with the currency and any other contents that may have currency fragments attached.

(e) If the currency was flat when mutilated, do not roll or fold the notes.

(f) If the currency was in a roll when mutilated, do not attempt to unroll or straighten it out."

"Supercritical Fluid Cleaning of Banknotes," *Industrial and Engineering Chemistry Research* 53 (January 15, 2014).

6. See John Deyell's excellent analysis of these countermarks, "Shroff Maarks on Bengal Sultans Tankas," February 2002, at Scott Semans World Coins, accessed July 15, 2014, http://coincoin.com/1068.htm.

7. Federal Register, https://www.federalregister.gov/articles/2014/05/29/2014-12435/exchange-of-mutilated-paper-currency, accessed August 21, 2014.

8. Delma K. Romines, *Hobo Nickels: An Extensive Study of Hobo Nickels* (Newbury Park, CA: Lonesome John Publishing Co., 1982).

9. Damaged money can be very fragile. The Bureau of Engraving and Printing

10. Edward Haller, "The Nature of Encrustation on Coins from the Wreck of the *Republic* (1865)," Odyssey Marine Exploration, 2013, accessed July 15, 2014, http://shipwreck.net/pdf/OMEPaper31-2013.pdf.

Further Reading

Ackroyd, Peter. *Newton*. New York: Nan A. Talese, 2008 ebook.

Anthon, Charles E. *American Journal of Numismatics and Bulletin of the American Numismatic and Archaeological Society* II (June 1867).

Bart, Frederick J. *United States Paper Money Errors: A Comprehensive Catalog and Price Guide*. Iola, WI: Krause Publications, 2008.

Brunk, Gregory G. *Merchant and Privately Countermarked Coins: Advertising on the World's Smallest Billboards*. 2nd ed. Rockford, IL: World Exonumia Press, 2003.

Chambers, Bruce W. *Old Money: American Trompe l'Oeil Images of Currency*. New York: Berry-Hill Galleries, 1988.

Colo, Papo, and Jeanette Ingberman. *Illegal America*. New York: Exit Art, 1982. (To open a new copy of this exhibition catalog, one has to tear an actual US dollar bill.)

Craig, Sir John. *Newton at the Mint*. Cambridge, UK: Cambridge University Press, 1946.

Frankenstein, Alfred. *After the Hunt: William Harnett and Other American Still Life Painters, 1870–1900*. Berkeley: University of California Press, 1969.

Goodwin, Jason. *Greenback: The Almighty Dollar and the Invention of America*. New York, Macmillan, 2003.

Griffith, J. H. *Money As It Was and Is*. New York: Eagle Job and Book Printing Department, 1877.

Gross, Gay Merrill. *Money-Gami*. New York: Parragon Books, 2014.

Herbert, Alan. *Official Price Guide to Mint Errors*. 6th ed. New York: Random House, 2002.

Margolis, Arnold. *The Error Coin Encyclopedia*. New York: published by author, 1991.

Prown, Jules David. "Mind in Matter: An Introduction to Material Culture Theory and Method." *Winterthur Portfolio* 17, no. 1 (Spring 1982): 1–19.

Romines, Delma K., *Hobo Nickels: An Extensive Study of Hobo Nickels*. Newbury Park, CA: Lonesome John Publishing, 1982.

Rosato, Angelo A. *Encyclopedia of the Modern Elongated*. New Milford, CT: Angros Publishers, 1990.

Sheldon, William H., MD, Dorothy I. Pascal, and Walter Breen. *Penny Whimsy: A Revision of Early American Cents, 1793–1814: An Exercise in Descriptive Classification with Tables of Rarity and Value*. New York: Harper and Brothers, 1958.

Shutty, Michael S., Jr. *One Coin Is Never Enough: Why and How We Collect*. Iola, WI: Krause Publications, 2011.

Spagnuolo, Peter. *Notes in Passing*. New York: Pavel Zoubok Gallery, 2008.

Vanselow, Clarence H., and Sherri R. Forrester, "Shell Thickness of the Copper-Clad Cent," *Journal of Chemical Education* 70 (1993).

Internet Sources

Americans for Common Cents: http://www.pennies.org

American Numismatic Association: http://www.money.org

American Numismatic Society: http://www.numismatics.org

The Combined Organizations of Numismatic Error Collectors of America: http://hermes.csd.net/~coneca/

Inspector Collector, author's website: http://www.inspectorcollector.com

Museum of American Finance, public programs presented by the author: http://www.moaf.org/education/classes/index

US government agencies

http://www.federalreserve.gov

http://www.moneyfactory.gov

http://www.secretservice.gov

http://www.treasury.gov

http://www.usmint.gov

Credits

Acknowledgments

E pluribus diversitas
(Out of many, diversity)

Writing this book has helped me cultivate rarity in coins, banknotes, and friends of a feather. I hope you, dear reader, have savored the preceding words and numbers that the following people have generously helped me round up.

Alex Kalman, diviner of the human footprint, IOU for being the first to suggest a book about mutilated money. I am also indebted to Princeton Architectural Press's acquisitions editor Sara Bader for her faith in this, my first book, and for her extraordinarily precise, wise, careful, and cordial editing, and that of her fellow editors Sara Stemen and Erica Olsen. Thanks also to Paul Wagner, Jan Haux, Mia Johnson, Janet Behning, and Andrea Chlad of Princeton Architectural Press. Thanks to Marty Heitner for his friendship and photography supreme, and to numismatist Michael Pfefferkorn for his deep knowledge, careful suggestions, and great kindness to a perfect stranger. Great gratitude is also due to Micki Watanabe Spiller, my better two-thirds, for providing backbone, technical ken, and artistic wizardry, and to our son Hiro, who also stooped to the occasion countless times, finding more "messed-up money" than anyone except his Grampa Mort and Aunt Lora.

Other contributors of mangled money over the years include John Beifuss, Adam Cooperman, Marc Labelle, Fred Senters, Dawn Sweetman, and Aaron Underwood. Artists who contributed mutilated money, creative money works, and concepts include: Martine Aballéa, J. S. G. Boggs, Gülşen Çalık, Jim Costanzo, Peggy Diggs, Nicolás Dumit Estévez, George Ferrandi, Dustin Grella, Gay Merrill Gross, David Greg Harth, Marko Burić Hindkjaer, David F. Jelinek, Adamandia Kapsalis, Lady Pink, Annie Lanzillotto, Hanne Lauridsen, Norm Magnusson, Jeff McMahon, Paul McMahon, Richard Minsky, Cyrilla Mozenter, *Por El Ojo* (Julia Balmaceda, Federico Gonzalez, Daniel Sanjurjo, Ignacio Sourrouille), Dread Scott, Susan Share, Karen Shaw, Robbin Ami Silverberg, Roger Smith, Jonathan Stangroom, Rumiko Tsuda, Mark Wagner, Beriah Wall, and Dolores Zorreguieta.

Thanks also to Khi Armand, Aaron Beebe, Kenneth H. Blumberg, David Brody, Patrick Burns, Dusan Canovic, Gaetano Carboni, Jonathan R. Cohen, David J. Cowen, Jeanne Driscoll, Jay Edlin, Douglas P. Evans, Jim Bob Evans, Michael Garofalo, Paul Glastris, Stephen Gould, Cheryl Greenacre, Joseph E. Kulba, Nabil M. Lawandy, Rosemary Lazenby, Dana "there is nothing wrong with your cite, but..." Louttit, Alec Mahrer, Sid Mandelbaum, Chris Meyers, Melissa M. Monroe, Kukiko Nobori, Henry Petroski, Peter Prescott, Sidney Rocke, Josh Safdie, Jill J. Underwood, Rob Van Erve, Steven V. Vella, Jonathan J. Ward, and Tsugie Watanabe.

About the Author